OXFORDSHIRE

Here
lieth the Body of
THOMAS HEARNE M.A.
Who ſtudied and preſerved
Antiquities, He died June 10ᵗʰ
1735 aged 57 years.

Deut: XXXII. 7
Remember the days of old, Conſider
the years of many generations: aſk
thy Father, and he will ſhew thee,
thy elders, and they will tell thee.

Job: VIII: 8: 9: 10:
For enquire, I pray thee, of the
former age, and prepare thy ſelf
to the ſearch of their fathers.

For we are but as yeſterday &
know nothing becauſe our days
upon earth are a ſhadow.

Shall not they teach thee, and
tell thee, and utter words out
of their heart.

Facies Averſae Tabulae in Cœmiterio D. Petri in Oriente Oar
exhibet hanc Inſcriptionem repertam A.D. MDCCLIV

The inscription on the tomb of Thomas Hearne who was buried in the
churchyard of St. Peter in the East, Oxford. (*Bodleian Library, G. A. Oxon.
a. 68, fol. 123*).

OXFORDSHIRE

A HANDBOOK
FOR STUDENTS OF LOCAL HISTORY

Edited by
D. M. Barratt
and
D G. Vaisey

BASIL BLACKWELL · OXFORD
FOR
OXFORDSHIRE RURAL COMMUNITY COUNCIL
1973

Printed in Great Britain by
Western Printing Services Ltd, Bristol
and bound by Kemp Hall Bindery, Oxford

List of Contents

List of Plates

The picture on the cover shows Witney at the end of the 18th century. The watercolour is ascribed to Paul Sandby. (*Victoria and Albert Museum, D. 915–1904; crown copyright*).

The editors are indebted to the Bodleian Library, Oxford for permission to reproduce the inscription inside the front cover and plates 1–7; to the Oxford Diocesan Registrar for plates 5 and 6; to the Priest-in-charge and Churchwardens of the parish of Mapledurham for plate 7; to the Cambridge University Committee for Aerial Photography for plate 8; to the Oxford City Libraries for plate 9; and to the Victoria and Albert Museum for the picture on the cover.

Preface

There has never been a time when local history has been the subject of such widespread interest. The Oxfordshire Rural Community Council's Standing Committee on Local History may claim to have played some part in stimulating this interest in the country parishes of the county. Since the Committee began its work in 1948, it has arranged exhibitions and talks in village halls and, to encourage those who are prepared to do more than look and listen, it has organized competitions for scrapbooks and memoirs. Its local correspondents have collected information for the Oxfordshire committee of the National Register of Archives and reported on discoveries and developments in their neighbourhoods. These were pioneer activities first undertaken when few outlets were available to the amateur historian anxious to find out more about the background of his own community.

Of recent years the situation has been transformed. There has been a remarkable increase in the publication of books, pamphlets and articles on local subjects; excellent opportunities are now provided by the City and County Museum and by the University Department for External Studies for study and participation in field work; expert advice is readily given by local history specialists in the County Record Office, the Bodleian and other libraries; local societies have multiplied, providing opportunities for members to take part in communal projects; children and young people from the primary school to the college of education are encouraged to study for themselves the history of their own environment.

Few people can now be unaware of the importance and the fascination of local history.

In the light of all these developments perhaps the most useful function of our Committee is now to provide a common meeting ground for representatives of all the bodies concerned with local history in the county where they can keep in touch with each other's activities and find ways of meeting new problems as they arise. The welcome news that the Rural Community Council would be able to make a grant towards the cost of publication has enabled the Committee to fill one long-felt need in the production of this *Handbook*. The growing scale and professionalism of local history studies can be daunting to a student in search of sources and advice about how to use them; even the contributors to the *Handbook*, with considerable experience in their own special subjects and departments, will be the first to acknowledge that they have learned much that is new to them from the contributions of their colleagues. We hope, therefore, that the *Handbook* will prove to be useful to all those working on Oxfordshire subjects, whether amateurs or professionals.

In describing the scope of the work, it may be useful first to explain what is not included in it. Its geographical limits are those of the county as it is in 1973, excluding the University and City of Oxford: it does not take account of impending changes in local government boundaries. It is not a guide-book: the forthcoming Oxfordshire volume in Professor Pevsner's *Buildings of England* will, no doubt, fill many gaps left by older publications. The examples of sites included in Part I have been chosen by way of illustration to the text. The book is concerned with history rather than archaeology; although reference is necessarily made to archaeological evidence in early periods, primarily the *Handbook* is concerned with written sources whether in print or manuscript. In the case of manuscript materials the information given is restricted to sources available within the county. These are unusually rich and unusually widely dispersed. To have attempted to include references to Oxfordshire materials in the Public Record Office or the British Museum would have added very considerably to the burden of compilers and readers alike.

The table of contents indicates the intended scope of the *Handbook*. The 'Introduction to Oxfordshire History' which constitutes the first section was initially included in the general plan for two reasons. The compilers hoped that it would enable those working on the history of a particular locality or period to see their chosen subject in a wider perspective. They also hoped that students who might be thinking of working on an Oxfordshire subject would welcome suggestions about problems calling for further study. The Committee is particularly grateful to Mrs. Maslen (formerly Miss M. Jones of the County Record Office) for undertaking the difficult task of combining and supplementing the material sent in by various contributors for this introduction. In her capable hands it not only fulfils its original purpose but forms a continuous and balanced study of the social and economic history of the county from the Roman occupation to the present day which will be widely welcomed. For many readers this will be the most interesting part of the *Handbook;* but we hope that the practical information given in the remaining sections will introduce the local historian to the essential tools of his trade, enabling him to satisfy his own curiosity about the history of his family, his house or his village, and perhaps to produce published work of lasting value to others.

For bringing this project to a successful conclusion we are particularly indebted to Dr. D. M. Barratt and Mr. D. G. Vaisey of the Department of Western Manuscripts in the Bodleian Library, who have revised and edited the text for publication. The text itself incorporates the work of a number of contributors, many of whom represent the libraries, museums and the record office on this Committee. We should also like to acknowledge very gratefully the helpful co-operation given by other advisers to whom we applied for information and suggestions. These include Mr. P. D. C. Brown of the Ashmolean Museum, Mrs. Pamela Horn and Mrs. M. L.

I

An Introduction to Oxfordshire History

I

Oxfordshire has been attractive to settlers from earliest times. The first artefacts found in the county belong to paleolithic days but the first farmers and permanent settlers were probably neolithic. Evidence for prehistoric settlements can be found in many parts of the county, although early farmers evidently preferred the gravels and loam of the Thames valley and established a pattern of settlement there which was followed for many centuries.

There was no sharp break in farming practice when the Romans came in the middle of the first century (A.D. 43) and without some distinctly Roman piece of pottery it is often not possible to decide that a settlement is Roman rather than pre-Roman in date. A wide variety of evidence is available for life in the country. On the river gravels along the Thames, a large number of ditched field-systems and subrectangular enclosures joined by ditched trackways have been identified by air photography. Examples at Langford Downs and Stanton Harcourt can be ascribed to the late Iron Age/early Roman period; at Long Wittenham, just over the river, to the first and second centuries; and on the gravels just north of Dorchester to the 3rd and 4th centuries. Considerable quantities of pottery from these ditches suggest that some sort of domestic activity must have taken place nearby, but there is no evidence of stone buildings, or of houses of great permanence.

Away from the river gravels the soils are not so suitable

for recording these ditch systems. Yet a number of stone build-ings have been located from the air. The most famous of these sites is the villa at Ditchley. This is a small stone house set in a walled yard with barns, a well and a threshing floor. The excavations suggest that the stone buildings replaced a wooden one at some date at the end of the 1st century. The main house at Ditchley was added to from time to time, and there were alterations to the farm buildings and to the immediately adjacent ditched enclosures. Quite a number of small farms of this type have been discovered, and some ex-cavated more or less satisfactorily: as at Worsham (in Asthall), Glympton, Islip, Wheatley, Burcot, Wigginton and Middle-ton Stoney. The current excavations at Shakenoak farm, on the border of Wilcote and North Leigh, promise to produce a better set of results than is at present available.

Large villas, more like country houses than farms, existed at North Leigh and Stonesfield. Both of these were equipped with mosaic pavements in the style of the 4th-century Corinium school. Such lavish houses probably represent the gradually accumulated wealth of several generations of pros-perous Romano-Britons.

Rural settlements rather than isolated houses and farms existed at a number of places, but they have been little ex-plored, and in no case is their full extent known. Asthall, Bloxham and Swalcliffe near Madmarston camp are examples of this type of settlement. At Swalcliffe the occupied area extends over 50 acres, twice as large as the walled area of Al-chester, although its importance, or status, was such that it was never enclosed within a wall. Here, as elsewhere in the county, the field name 'Blacklands' – black due to the accumulated organic debris of early settlement – is a clue to the ancient site.

Dorchester and Alchester (near Bicester) were the towns of Roman Oxfordshire. Both grew upon the sites of the immediate pre-Roman inhabitants of the area, the Belgae, and it is probable that both began life as forts. Dorchester stands on the Thames at its junction with the river Thame, and at the crossing of the road running northwards from

Silchester to Watling Street and Leicester. Alchester is situated on the same north–south road, at its crossing with the east-west road from Verulamium to Cirencester. The northern and western half of the county formed part of the tribal area of the Dobunni, the southern and eastern of the Catuvellanni. With the advance of the Roman army further into Britain, Dorchester and Alchester were left for settlement by civilians, and it is no doubt due to their positions and to the communications which grew up around them that they flourished, presumably as local market towns. Both were eventually defended by walls and ramparts.

A Roman-Celtic temple at Woodeaton, with the familiar double square plan, is the only temple so far found in the county. The site is remarkable for the number of small objects which have been picked up there, so many that it has been suggested that an annual fair and market was held there.

The area now occupied by Oxford itself was no more than ordinary valley farmland, but the surrounding hills produced the raw materials, timber and clay, for making pottery. The remains of potters' workshops have been found at Headington, Cowley, Rose Hill, Shotover and Horspath. The industry seems to have been producing for local distribution by the end of the 1st century, and throughout the 2nd. But in the 3rd and 4th centuries the output and distribution increased. Mortaria, the gritted mixing bowls, and red pottery imitating the samian ware by then obtainable were being made and exported throughout southern Britain, from Richborough in Kent to Segontium in North Wales.

II

The collapse of Roman rule after A.D. 410 left the region open to the Anglo-Saxon invaders. There is little evidence as yet to show whether they made use of the farms and villages of their predecessors; in general it has not been possible to link the Roman site in a parish such as Wigginton or Middleton Stoney with the later Anglo-Saxon village. Excavations at

Dorchester and at Shakenoak in North Leigh are exciting in suggesting continuity on some of the Thames valley sites: there were German mercenaries in both places in the 5th century and later Anglo-Saxon occupation. British victories in the early 6th century possibly account for the scarcity of early Anglo-Saxon place-names on the Oxfordshire side of the Thames, but there are signs in the New Wintles Farm site at Eynsham of late 5th- and early 6th-century Saxon occupation. With the recapture of Benson and Eynsham in 571, recorded by the Anglo-Saxon Chronicle, permanent English settlement could go ahead.

Archaeology and the careful study of village siting show the routes which the main groups of invaders took. The Saxons moved from the south and east up from Hampshire or along the Thames and its tributaries. The Angles came from the north-east along the Chilterns and the Icknield way, or from the Midlands, like the Middle Angle people, the Huicce, who moved westwards into Oxfordshire and have left their name in Wychwood. The student of place-names and the archaeologist can only very occasionally distinguish between the Anglian and Saxon elements in Oxfordshire villages, but the political history of the kingdom set up shows the conflicting pulls of the South and Midlands. At first the West Saxon kingdom controlled the Thames and the lands north of it, but by the 7th and 8th centuries the Anglian kingdom of Mercia ruled as far south as Wiltshire and Berkshire, and in 674 the Mercian court was at Thame. The rise of Wessex in the 9th and 10th centuries and in the fight against the Danes re-established its political control over the region, but Mercian law and custom remained the strongest influence north of the Thames. At the end of the 10th century Woodstock, a favourite royal hunting lodge, was said to be in the land of the Mercians. Though the wars against the Danes took place on the borders there are few detectable Danish elements in Oxfordshire history, save for the names of a few Danish landowners and for the presence of Danes in Oxford itself in the early 11th century.

From the 10th and 11th centuries it is possible to speak of

the county of Oxford. Oxford was laid out in the early 10th century as one of the Wessex burhs in the drive against the Danes, and the lands of the shire were attached to it. It was the only county town apart from Dorchester, which had few pretensions by this time. Early royal estates, pre-eminently Benson, or bishopric estates such as Thame were the important local centres of government. They gave their names to the hundred districts which were organized in the 11th and 12th centuries, although the beginning of their courts and the hundredal meeting places such as 'speech hill' in Bletchingdon for the southern half of Ploughley may go back to far earlier times. The county boundary and the administrative districts of the late Saxon and early Norman period were to exist for the next thousand years.

New landlords came into the county after the Norman Conquest and created the 'feudal Oxfordshire' of honours, knights and castles. The impact can be seen in a village such as Ascott under Wychwood where there are remains of the 12th-century motte and bailey castle at Ascot Earl, and where Ascot D'Oyley bears the name of its Norman lord, Robert D'Oilley who was the Conqueror's chief agent in Oxfordshire, the builder of Oxford castle and the lord of the honour of Hook Norton. Few of the great baronies or honours had their main castle in Oxfordshire, but many great lords held land and endowed their knights with local manors. The earl of Chester for instance had tenants at Pyrton whose other holdings were on his Chester lands, and whose obligation in return for their Oxfordshire holdings was to be in the van of the army going into Wales. These lords and under-tenants with their involved family relationships, as well as the intricate manorial descents of their holdings, deserve study. Their fortunes and policies influenced the lot of many villages and their peasant farmers. They brought Oxfordshire into the politics of the age. The under-tenants were the men who ran local government for the king from the late 12th century as jurors, coroners, escheators, assessors of taxes, and from the late 13th century as members of parliament: the Elsfields, the Brulys of Waterstock, the Harcourts, the Fettiplaces and many

B

others. The history of the honour of Wallingford illuminates some of this little-remembered feudal world. It held many manors in the south of the county and its lord's stand for Matilda embroiled the Thames region in the anarchy of Stephen's reign, when the king held Oxford and built Crowmarsh Gifford castle to counter Wallingford. The castle at Britwell was defended by Stephen's supporters against Henry Plantagenet in 1153 and was presumably one of the many castles pulled down in Oxfordshire when Henry came to the throne. Wallingford honour itself passed into royal hands. Courts were held for its manors and hundreds in the south of the county not only throughout the Middle Ages, but also after 1540 when it became Ewelme honour. They were continued as late as the 19th century.

The chief influence on the medieval county was undoubtedly royal. The king's government continued to expand into more aspects of local life through its taxes, courts and inquiries. The kings themselves came into Oxfordshire to the royal forests, to the hunting lodge at Woodstock or to the palace at Beaumont in Oxford and in the later Middle Ages to the new palace at Ewelme. Royal estates were generally granted out, but other Oxfordshire estates came into crown hands for varying periods and can be traced in the public records. Oxford itself saw a number of critical councils and parliaments held there in the 13th century, but although directly involved in national problems in this and later centuries the county was markedly loyal. Henry III's Oxford Parliament of 1258, for example, ushered in the baronial wars but he was able to move against De Montfort from Oxford in 1264. Edward II's favourite Piers Gaveston brought disturbances to north Oxfordshire in the early 14th century; in 1387 the favourite of Richard II, De Vere, the earl of Oxford, was defeated at Radcot Bridge: in both cases the county's connection with the events has aptly been called incidental. In the 15th century the large royal estates secured by the succession of the Lancastrians again ensured the loyalty of landowners, among them the De Veres, the De La Poles of Ewelme, and the Lovels of Minster Lovell fame. The economic and social problems of this period were felt in Oxfordshire villages as much as anywhere, but there were no serious revolts in the county in the 14th century, although there were riots nearby at Abingdon. It was a pattern of political quiescence which remained largely undisturbed until the 17th century.

The most permanent memorial of the Anglo-Saxon and medieval period may well be the county's villages. By 1086 most of these had been settled; some more were added in the 12th and 13th centuries, but very few in the next six hundred years. Place-names are still the main sources for the earliest clearing, cultivation and settlement, although the archaeologist and aerial photographer are increasingly able to produce other kinds of evidence. Early charters record some villages as in the 10th-century grant of 20 hides in Tadmarton with its implication of open fields already laid out, but most places appeared on record for the first time in Domesday book in 1086. Historians and geographers have worked intensively on this great survey of lands. Its evidence is not easy to interpret, but the local historian's knowledge of local conditions and possible land usage can help towards understanding it. The survey shows that in the preceding centuries Oxford had become one of the most important towns in England, and Oxfordshire the second richest shire, with well-cultivated farms, rich pasture and meadow in the valleys, and woodland with pannage for pigs. Bampton was a prosperous market town, and in the Banbury and Thames valley regions the population was dense by medieval standards.

Records, excavations, field work and aerial photography continue to provide evidence of growth in the two centuries after Domesday. They show new expansion in the village itself, new hamlets in the parish and land newly brought under the plough to feed a population which at least trebled itself in many places. This is the period of the clearings or assarts which created Leafield in Wychwood forest and Hailey from assart land in Witney, and of assarts on the Chilterns which made that sparsely populated region more habitable for new settlers in Nuffield and Nettlebed and in farms in clearings above Watlington. Even marshy Otmoor was used more intensively by the seven villages around it. Landlords were interested in encouraging towns and markets. Henry II made the new borough of Woodstock, the Bishop of Lincoln the new towns of Banbury and Thame, the Bishop of Winchester Witney; the development of Henley in the same period still needs study. Markets flourished at Deddington, Banbury, Bicester, Chipping Norton and Henley and in Oxford itself.

The county's prosperity depended on farming and in the 12th and 13th centuries the lords, particularly the ecclesiastics, exploited their farms and manorial rights intensively. Farming was mixed, sheep pasture and corn husbandry, and the balance between the two was not always easy. Population growth and the demand for grain put pressure on pasture for sheep as the 13th century wore on. When manorial documents become more plentiful it is possible to trace this in the bye-laws and in the actions for trespass. Wool was in demand abroad: Oseney Abbey traded with the Italians, the Bishop of Lincoln kept flocks on his manor of Banbury, and many lesser men must have shared in the trade. The arable was in open fields for the most part. How, why, and when this came to be are intriguing problems. The Oxfordshire evidence for the topography, regulation and division of the fields of individual villages could help to provide some answers not only for the 12th and 13th centuries but for as long as the fields were in existence. It has been suggested, for example, that there was a period of nomadic pastoral life in the early history of Oxfordshire settlers before they cultivated the arable and made the fields; or again that some of the intricate subdivisions of the open fields were only created with the growth of population in the 12th and 13th centuries. There is much, too, that the historian would like to know about the peasant farmer. In Domesday book about half the recorded population were *villani*, and the rest were mostly bordars or serfs; only 26 were freemen. There were many more freemen at the end of the 13th century, and there was a complicated land market, but there are many questions to be answered about the comparative prosperity or poverty of the still numerous villeins and cottagers in an age of land hunger, subdivision of farms, and manorialization. The claims of a lord were still a force to be reckoned with if hard times came.

There are over one hundred deserted and shrunken villages in Oxfordshire to testify to the changes that came over the county from the 14th century. Tusmore is the classic example of a village depopulated by the Black Death, the traditional explanation; Tilgarsley in Eynsham suffered a similar fate; and many Oxfordshire villages and hamlets showed the effects of plague in the 14th century in vacant tenements and tax abatements. But researchers emphasize that there were also other reasons for the death of a village, and it is wise to look further than rats and fleas. At the most thoroughly investigated site, Seacourt near Wytham, it looks as if the village was declining early in the 14th century because of bad weather and the original poor siting of the village. Here as elsewhere the decline can be traced over a long period of varying fortunes, in which plague was only one factor. At Brookend in Chastleton, no more than marginal land, the abbot of Eynsham fought hard in the 15th century to persuade tenants to take up vacant holdings and to keep the village from falling into ruins, but to no avail, and by 1469 it was virtually abandoned. Chilworth and Combe in Great Milton disappeared at the end of the 15th century under pressure from sheep farmers and enclosers, a common fate for hamlets in this area. It is clear that in Oxfordshire as elsewhere in England the marginal arable land, often the assarts of a previous generation, was going out of cultivation. One of the factors was the marked decline in the rural population of the county which affected the land market and wages and prices. Another factor was the policy of great landowners faced with higher wages, more demanding tenants and low grain prices.

By the 15th century abbeys like Thame, Dorchester or Abingdon, as well as great secular lords, preferred to lease rather than to farm their land directly. The break-up of manorial authority can be seen in Oxfordshire court rolls, and it contributed to the ease with which villeins could commute their services and gain greater freedom. Some small peasant families built up their family fortunes and it is possible to trace many Oxfordshire yeoman families from this period. But the enterprising men were those, often of the knightly class, who could take advantage of yet another factor in the situation, that is, the market for wool. The Danvers, Stonors and Dormers were three of the successful families who enclosed and invested in wool and sheep and cattle. Brasses and monuments in churches in Thame, Witney, Great Milton and elsewhere commemorate the lives of such men; the houses which they built can still be seen, and the fields which they enclosed and hedged can be found in many parts of the county. The regions between Thame and Dorchester, around Pyrton and in Wootton hundred were the most affected by this early enclosure. The county's complaints about the enclosers are recorded in the Domesday of Inclosures of 1517, but the movement continued throughout the 16th and 17th centuries.

County towns felt the chill winds of economic depression. Oxford's prospects as a cloth town were destroyed in the 13th century, apparently not so much from competition from the country weavers as from international competition from the Netherlands; it found some compensation in the growth of the University. Banbury went through a period of regression in the 14th century and Witney suffered in the Black Death. Yet by the 15th and early 16th centuries there is evidence of recovery shown in new buildings and prosperous town houses. Banbury's rise as a local centre is marked in the 15th century when the wool of the south Midlands was collected there. Henley prospered on its carrying trade by the Thames to London. Chipping Norton and Witney flourished on Cotswold wool and the growing export of cloth. Thame had its market and wealthy merchants with London connections. However, compared to other parts of the South and Midlands, a study of lay and clerical wealth has shown that Oxfordshire's growth rate had slowed down, and that by 1524 the county had fallen since Domesday from second to thirteenth place in the ranking of wealthy counties.

The fortunes of the church in medieval Oxfordshire were closely geared to those of the lay world. The missionary bishop Birinus was established at Dorchester in 634 under the patronage of the kings of Wessex. Politics dictated the later migrations of the bishopric: to Winchester in the heartland of Wessex by 660; then under Mercian rule back to Dorchester for a short time, and afterwards to Lichfield and Leicester. Although Dorchester was again the home of the bishop just before the Conquest, the Normans decided that the larger Midland centre of Lincoln would be more suitable, and Bishop Remigius moved the see there at the end of the 11th century. Despite the cross-country journey Oxfordshire remained under Lincoln until Henry VIII founded the diocese of Oxford. Remoteness from Lincoln was one of the factors in the rise of the University in Oxford; for the county it meant that a cathedral was never the focus of church life in it. Nonetheless the bishops had wealthy estates in the county, often visited Thame and Dorchester and had an influence on the medieval county second only to the king.

In the Anglo-Saxon period the earliest churches as at Bampton or Adderbury were centres for the whole area around them, and only gradually were village churches endowed: the large number of dependent chapelries in some areas, as in the villages around Dorchester, are survivals of this earlier system. There is little evidence either in documents or in surviving buildings to show in most cases when the local church was founded, though it is often suspected that it was in being by the time of Domesday. In the following centuries, it is sometimes possible to trace the fortunes of the parish churches in the Lincoln registers and later on in visitation records, although the most abundant evidence, from parish records, is not available until after 1500 or often 1600. The fabric of the parish church itself is usually the best guide to its medieval fortunes: with the expansion of the 12th and 13th centuries new chapels were built and additions and alterations were made to existing churches. Some churches disappeared with their villages in the 14th century, but new men were often generous, and 14th- and 15th-century chantries and chapels in Banbury, Witney and Thame, for example, confirm the picture of renewed prosperity. Their charities, too, are revealing: Richard Quatremains, merchant of London, member of parliament and High Sheriff of Oxfordshire, founded not only the chapel at Rycote but also almshouses at Thame. There are other notable examples in the county, in particular at Ewelme. Gifts and endowments to the church in wills show the strength of lay piety in the century before the Reformation.

There were never many important monasteries in the county. One of the most influential was the great Benedictine Abbey of Abingdon just over the border: it is even suggested that there may have been a Christian community there before the usually accepted date of 700, which might provide a link with earlier Christian activity in the area. In Oxfordshire itself St. Frideswide's and Eynsham were pre-Conquest houses which continued to play an important part in later religious and economic life. Dorchester, though it ceased to be the centre of diocesan life, remained a religious house with regular canons. The only two Cistercian houses in the county were Thame and Bruern with Rewley as a house of studies in Oxford itself. Among the Oxford houses Oseney was preeminent in its influence as a landowner in the county as well as in the city; and the Oxford colleges were religious foundations with local estates. The economic as well as the religious rôle of these and many other smaller foundations of priories in the county was important in Oxfordshire history and can be traced in their cartularies and court rolls and in the Lincoln records.

III

Although we are told that Oxfordshire religious houses were not remarkable for wealth, learning or piety, their dissolution makes a natural starting-point for a survey of the county in the 16th and 17th centuries. Some monastic properties were used to provide or augment the endowments of Oxford colleges and their records passed with them into college muniment rooms, St. Frideswide's cartulary to Christ Church, for example, or St. John the Baptist's cartulary to Magdalen. In the printed cartularies published by the Oxford Historical Society, the editors have, in some cases, traced the post-dissolution history of monastic properties transferred to colleges and a sense of continuity has been preserved. But in Oxfordshire, as elsewhere, monastic wealth was also widely dispersed into private lay hands. Many county families, whose wealth is attested by their great houses and splendid tombs, owed their fortunes to the spoils of the monasteries. The outstanding example of an Oxfordshire magnate for whom the Tudor regime brought prosperity was Lord Williams of Thame, whose two daughters and co-heiresses married respectively Lord Norreys of Rycote and Sir Thomas Wenman of Thame. As lords lieutenant, deputy lieutenants, members of parliament and justices of the peace, such families continued to dominate the county for 200 years and more, surviving the Civil War and Interregnum with remarkable resilience. No one has yet made a detailed study of their wealth and influence; there is no book comparable with Dr. Mary Finch's *Five Northamptonshire families*. This would be a profitable field of investigation. It would be less easy but even more interesting to trace the fortunes of yeoman families, merchants and townsmen. There is some solid evidence of their rising standard of living in the good stone-built town and village houses dating from the late 16th and early 17th centuries; and in the wills and inventories surviving in large numbers in the local probate records now in the Bodleian.

But if the period brought increased prosperity to some, many were its victims. Changes in ownership of land helped to accelerate changes in estate management which would in any case have resulted from inflation and the pressures of a growing population. It was an age when landowners sought to exploit the resources of their property to the full, whether this entailed conversion from arable to pasture, enclosure of the commons, destruction of woodland, development of quarries or the search for minerals. In the latter part of the 16th century, suffering and unrest were intensified by years

of bad harvest, depression in the cloth industry and inflation-
ary prices. The unsuccessful rising on Enslow Hill (in Bletchingdon) in 1596 no doubt shows only the tip of the iceberg.
Of the pressure of increased population we have only indi-
rect evidence, for example, in the building of unlicensed cottages on the edges of forest land, and in the difficulty of
enforcing statutes against taking in lodgers. Court rolls are
the main source of information for these things; perhaps, as
our techniques improve, it will be possible to make fuller use
of early parish registers.

The trend of historical studies in the recent past has made
us more aware of the economic framework of local society
than of the character of the people who composed it. Yet the
16th and 17th centuries were pre-eminently ages of creative
thinking and criticism, when the invention of cheap printing
and the rapid increase of literacy made it easier for ideas to
spread. Evidence of the ways in which people's minds were
working is harder to find than evidence of the number of
chairs and tables they possessed; but it is worth pursuing. The
social and economic changes described above did not pass
without comment from thoughtful Elizabethan observers,
many of whom were inspired to make surveys of their own
counties. In Oxfordshire we are not so fortunate, but relevant
references may be found in Leland or Harrison, and Anthony
Wood's *Life and Times* has much incidental information
about the countryside he knew. Evidence of a very different
kind can be found in the depositions of witnesses in legal
actions, one of the few authentic records of the voice of the
common man. Although the 1596 rising failed, the ideas
which gave rise to it are illuminated for us by the examination of witnesses.

On religious issues the county was sharply divided with a
strong Puritan element in the north of the county, and a
vigorously sustained Catholic tradition in the south-east. The
north Oxfordshire preachers' sermons which have survived
in print, especially perhaps the sermons of Robert Harris of
Hanwell, have much to tell us of the attitudes and problems of
rural congregations. The inter-relation of economic unrest,

religious conviction and political alignment is a never-ending source of interest to historians of the 17th century. It is a subject which badly needs further study on a regional basis. Certainly north Oxfordshire was regarded by the Elizabethan and Stuart establishment as a particularly sensitive area. We may remember the parts played by Sir Anthony Cope and the Wentworth brothers in the Elizabethan House of Commons, or by Lord Saye and Sele in stimulating opposition to Stuart taxation and in making Broughton a focal point in planning the strategy of the Long Parliament. The Civil War came as the climax of a long period of unrest. With the establishment of the royal headquarters in Oxford the city became the inevitable target for the parliamentary attack, and heavy demands were made by both armies upon the resources of the surrounding countryside; there can have been few villages in the county which escaped the impact of the war. There must surely be more evidence for the local historian to find, if not on the military side, then of the administrative and social changes which so profoundly affected the local community during the Interregnum.

IV

The divisions in the county still marked local life in the 18th and 19th centuries. Banbury remained the centre of nonconformity in religion and politics. There was, for example, a vigorous Quaker movement in the town in the later 17th century and the most important Quaker meetings in the county were at Banbury and nearby villages such as the Sibfords and Shutford. A different type of nonconformity flourished in Bicester where the present Congregationalist church can trace a continuous history back to the late 17th century, and has been variously served by Presbyterians, Independents and Congregationalists. Witney warmly welcomed John Wesley, and soon became the chief stronghold of Methodism in the county outside Oxford itself. Catholic families survived quietly in the south and east, making a distinctive contribution to village life and often to agricultural progress: the Fermors of Tusmore, the Daveys of Overy whom George III, 'Farmer George', visited, the Simeons and Welds of Pyrton and Britwell, the Blounts of Mapledurham, and the Stonors in the Chilterns.

There was general acceptance of the Restoration and its political code. Few were non-jurors after 1688, and although the country squires were suspected of Jacobitism in the 18th century they did not want political upheaval. The famous 1754 Oxfordshire election celebrated as 'Jacobitism's last fling' showed the emotional hold of the 'old interest' on the county. It showed even more clearly the grasp of the great county families on politics, and the subsequent decision to debar long-lease tenants from voting effectively restricted the county electorate. By the 18th century the prominent names in Oxfordshire were Churchill, Dashwood, Lee, Bertie, North and Parker. The arrival of the Duke of Marlborough at Blenheim had brought a great magnate into county and city life, while the establishment of the Norths at Wroxton modified the radical tradition of Banbury borough. Parliamentary elections up to 1832 showed the importance of the political alignments and family connections of the county families in determining the swing between Tory and Whig. Nor did this influence disappear with the creation of new electorates from 1832 onwards, as any study of campaigns in the 19th and 20th centuries, whether for local or parliamentary elections, would show.

The social and economic rôle of these great families is as important a study for the 18th and 19th centuries as for the sixteenth. Richard Davis's map of the county in 1797 gives a vivid impression of great houses in the countryside with their gardens, parks and enclosures around them. A great deal of building was done in the 18th century, notably at Blenheim and Ditchley. In one way Oxfordshire can be said to have inspired the rest of England, for it was at Rousham in the 1730s that William Kent reacted against the formality of the 17th-century garden and was inspired with the idea of the English landscape garden. A number of landscape gardeners worked in Oxfordshire, and Blenheim is perhaps the best-known work of the most famous of them, Capability Brown. The landscape craze often involved drastic change, as at Nuneham Courtenay where the removal of the village to make Lord Harcourt's landscape garden is recognized as a germ of Oliver Goldsmith's 'The Deserted Village'. We may think, however, that the ordinary Oxfordshire man was more affected by the work provided in the big houses and on their estates: the bills and accounts of Ditchley, Wroxton or Nuneham show the servants, craftsmen, traders and labourers employed, and the life of a great house in its heyday. The 1851 census returns also show the employment provided on the landed estates. Estate policy and attitudes to issues such as enclosure and tithe commutation were of paramount importance in an agricultural county. As tenant farming became widespread from the late 18th century there is much to be learnt from estate leases and accounts of the varying fortunes of the Oxfordshire farmer in the 18th and 19th centuries. Arthur Young in his *View of the agriculture of Oxfordshire* (1809) and Boyd Orr a century later, in his survey of *Agriculture in Oxfordshire* (1916), both stressed the need for enlightened guidance from landowners. Boyd Orr regarded their attitudes to rents and capital improvements as a major factor in 19th- and early 20th-century Oxfordshire farming. In the crises caused by cattle plague in 1865 and by the national slump in wheat and grain prices after 1870, much depended on how far landlords could reduce rents or help with expensive conversions to dairying.

Oxfordshire farmers have had many challenges to meet in the last two centuries, not only from national and international movements of prices and demand, and competition from farms abroad and in the colonies, but also from local changes in communications and in agriculture. Turnpike trusts and enclosure awards brought the modern, pre-motorway, road system into being by the early 19th century. Navigation on the Thames was improved in the 17th and 18th centuries, and by the end of the 18th century the Oxford canal was completed. Half a century later in 1844, and after much heart-searching, the Great Western Railway was allowed to enter Oxford, and many other railway schemes followed, some carried out and others not. Access to these improved means of transport helped many farmers to cater for the growing markets of London and the Midlands. They encouraged the dairy farming of the Thames valley region and specialized industries such as that of watercress-growing at Ewelme. On the other hand Boyd Orr attributed the conservatism in agriculture in the north-west of the county, in small places like Epwell, Balscot, Shenington, Alkerton and Hornton, to the lack of good railways and roads, which meant that they had no easy access to Banbury market for their produce, or for the profitable carriage of feeding stuff and manure to their farms.

By far the greatest change in the county's agriculture and landscape was brought about by the parliamentary enclosure of the 18th and 19th centuries. About 40 per cent of Oxfordshire's arable was still open-field at the beginning of this process. Young spoke of the 'Goths and Vandals' of the open fields in his survey of the county, but modern historians are less contemptuous. A study of Oxfordshire wills and inventories, confirmed by other records, has shown that there were many improvements within open-field farming in the 16th and 17th centuries: by leys farming or convertible husbandry, especially in the northern parishes; or by new divisions of the fields, again illustrated in the north where two fields had often been divided into four quarters by this period; or by experiments in sowing different crops either on an individual or a village basis. The splendid series of enclosure acts, awards and maps for Oxfordshire villages repay close study for a better understanding of both the causes and the effects of enclosure. It was not always a simple case of improving open-field farming. In some instances enclosure was a rationalization of holdings already accumulated by a few farmers; in others it came from a desire to bring wastes and common into cultivation. The reasons for postponing enclosure are interesting too. The most spectacular instance was at Otmoor with its riots in 1830, but commoners and tithe owners also waged less violent battles in other places.

On the whole north Oxfordshire parishes were amongst the earliest enclosures of the 18th century, while some of the latest in the 19th century are found on and around the Chilterns in the south of the county. Crowell open fields were only enclosed in 1881, almost within living memory. Relics of common meadow can still be seen in Yarnton lot meadow. The enclosure awards themselves are still in daily use to establish rights, roads, footpaths and commons.

There have been many commentators on the changes in Oxfordshire rural society of this period, on such matters as the disappearance of the small landowner, the rise of the tenant farmer and the distress of the agricultural labourer. The Oxfordshire scene was not unique, but since it was one of the rural counties most affected by parliamentary enclosure the connection between enclosure and these changes has to be considered. Historians now think that the years from the mid-17th to the mid-18th centuries were the crucial ones for the decline of the small Oxfordshire farmers. Enclosure acts and awards used with land tax assessments show that the small owner-occupier was on the way out in some parishes before parliamentary enclosure could have brought about his demise. On the other hand he survived in some other parishes well into the 19th century. How far enclosure was the main culprit in causing rural distress is again debated, and doubted. The great variety of situations revealed in the enclosure awards make some hardships and injustice indubitable. Yet researchers point to parishes where the enclosers tried to be fair to all concerned; and there are factors of population increase and lack of industrialization in the county as well as inadequate holdings to be considered among the causes of poverty.

The problems of the Oxfordshire poor can hardly be denied in the face of the long lists and cases both in the parish records of the overseers of the poor and in the justices' records at Quarter Sessions, which begin for the county in 1687. Nearly every parish showed increased expenditure on poor relief between 1780 and 1830, particularly over the period of the French wars. A variety of schemes were tried out, from child allowances to the Speenhamland and roundsmen schemes, all of which bore heavily on the rates of the individual parish. Landowners turned with relief to the Poor Law Unions after 1834, which usually reduced the rates but not the problem. Some workers sought to ease their bitter frustration by participation in the desperate labourers' revolt of 1830, the so-called 'Swing' riots; others, as at Otmoor, fiercely opposed the enclosure movement. Forty-two years later their descendants took part in the first attempt to create a national union for agricultural labourers. In the 1840's Oxfordshire shared in the utopian agrarian schemes of the Chartist leader, Feargus O'Connor, and his National Land Company, and Charterville for smallholders was set up on an estate at Minster Lovell in 1847, with a house, stable and pigsty for each occupier. All but two smallholders soon left. Migration was another remedy for the poor in the 19th century, and local studies would be useful: figures suggest that early in the 19th century up to one third of the natural increase in Oxfordshire's population migrated to other areas in Britain. Later in the century there was emigration abroad, for example from Bicester to the United States in 1830, and from Milton under Wychwood to New Zealand in a party led by the redoubtable Christopher Holloway in 1873. There was little improvement for the agricultural worker over the century. In 1801 the census showed that thirty per cent of all the county's inhabitants were employed 'chiefly in agriculture', and in the 1911 census agricultural labourers still formed over one-quarter of Oxfordshire's total male work force, but their wage in the first decade of the 20th century was one of the lowest in the country. It was a reflection generally of the depressed state of farming in the county between 1870 and the first world war.

Many of the county's problems were tackled by new bodies after 1832, the year which ushered in not only parliamentary reform but a period of experiment in local government. Local sanitary and highway boards, and Poor Law Unions and school boards have left records, many yet to be worked on by researchers. School log books, for example, show vividly the hardships of village schoolteachers at the beginning of a century of universal education. In 1888 the County Council was set up and took over many administrative functions from Quarter Sessions, which up to that time had been 'the maid of all work' for county administration. The period of County Council administration itself can soon become a subject of historical research.

The church was another institution which saw many changes in the 19th century. The inadequacies of the 18th-century church have often been exaggerated, and in Thomas Secker Oxford had from 1737 to 1758 a worthy and efficient bishop much concerned with all aspects of parish welfare. Nevertheless, by 1780 about 60 per cent of Oxfordshire parishes were without a resident rector or vicar, and were served only by a curate usually with an inadequate stipend. Most of these non-residents were pluralists, but in some instances there was no adequate parsonage house in which an incumbent could reside. One type of 18th-century non-residence was peculiar to the areas round the two great universities: college livings near Oxford such as Garsington, Stanton St. John or Bletchingdon were usually at this period served by fellows resident in college acting either as incumbents or as curates to other non-residents. Inspections of parish churches carried out by Archdeacon John Potter between 1755 and 1759 reveal a sorry picture of neglected church fabrics and fittings. By the end of the century there were populous parishes with very insufficient church accommodation, and some newly developed areas of settlement with no church at all. Most of these problems were dealt with by 19th-century legislation, but in the diocese of Oxford reforms were carried out with particular vigour and thoroughness by the famous Samuel Wilberforce, 'the remodeller of the episcopate', who was bishop from 1845 to 1869. By the end of his episcopate virtually every village had a resident parson (modern unions of small and poor benefices were only just beginning) who devoted most of his time to pastoral work and study. With the aid of Wilberforce's Diocesan Church Building Society new churches were built, and new parishes

C

formed, in most of the areas of greatest need, notably on the outskirts of Oxford, Banbury, Witney and Henley; numerous new parsonage houses were built, and older houses enlarged. A vast programme of church restoration was undertaken, and the influence of the Oxford Movement could also be seen in more frequent church services and more seemly church fittings. Oxfordshire is fortunate in that these changing patterns of church life can be followed in detail for each individual parish from a remarkable series of clergy's answers to bishops' visitation questionnaires which run from 1738 to the 20th century.

Parish records and visitation returns help to build up a picture of much more than just church life. Before the age of the car, truck and lorry, Oxfordshire was a county of small communities with local craftsmen and shopkeepers. Many villages were at their most populous in the mid-19th century and feast days and fairs were important. Local church, school and squire continue to feature largely in early 20th-century recollections of rural life, such as Flora Thompson's *Lark Rise to Candleford*. Apart from Oxford itself, Banbury is the community best served by its local historians, although the picture of 19th-century life there is perhaps not typical of other less industrialized and more conformist towns. The study of Bicester in the 17th and 18th centuries drawn for us from local wills and inventories has still to be paralleled by similar studies of other market towns. There is much work that can be done in recreating the communities of towns and villages in 19th- and early 20th-century Oxfordshire from records which are often more easily handled by the amateur than those of earlier centuries. County directories and newspapers often provide a good starting point, while the government census returns, particularly those from 1851 and later decades, as they are opened to the public, are full of invaluable information on families, work, migration into and out of the district and other subjects. Family photographs and letters, and personal recollections, as well as the study of the vast number of legal and administrative documents surviving for this period all make research more fruitful.

One of the great changes to be recorded in Oxfordshire villages in the 20th century is in the kind of work available to their inhabitants. In the Middle Ages the main industries in the county apart from agriculture were quarrying and cloth-making, and both survived into modern times. The stone quarried at Headington, Bladon, Taynton and Burford, and the slates at Stonesfield were worked by a succession of craftsmen whose services have been in demand far beyond Oxfordshire. But neither these crafts nor the smaller industries like brick-making, nor the specialized town occupations, could absorb those who found no work on the land. In the mid-18th century the manufacture of shag or plush spread rapidly in villages around Banbury, benefitting from the earlier girth, web and horse-cloth trade, but it contracted again slowly from the mid-19th century onwards under competition from Coventry's power looms. Lacemaking was another industry which failed to meet Midland competition: in the 19th century it was a cottage industry providing additional income to many a labourer's family; the 1871 census recorded over 1000 female lacemakers in Oxfordshire, most of them in the Chiltern parishes and on the Buckinghamshire borders. A similar cottage industry, glovemaking, which flourished in and around Woodstock, has survived on a limited scale. At Witney the blanket industry has not merely survived: it has expanded because it was successfully adapted to the machine age. The other successful industrial venture in 19th-century Oxfordshire was at Banbury. Prosperous agricultural-implement makers are found there in the early years of the century, and in 1846 Bernhard Samuelson set up the Britannia Works which employed about 300 people in 1859. Other industries in the county have been minor: clock-making, bell-founding, paper-making, boat-building, and ropemaking. Brewing, of course, occupied many a local worthy; Oxfordshire court rolls are full of brewers and tipplers, but as an industry it was most important in the rise of Henley. William Morris's bicycle business established in the last years of the 19th century was destined to alter Oxford and Oxfordshire more than any other in its history; the rise of Morris's motor works at Cowley has been the biggest factor in changing employment and life generally in the county.

Oxfordshire has been fortunate in keeping much of its rural character both in its villages and smaller towns longer than some southern and midland counties. Its villages have only slowly become dormitories for London, the Midlands and Oxford itself; or in other cases the modern equivalent of the medieval shrunken village. The mechanization of farming and the break-up of the great landed estates in the county have changed farming: hedgerows are fast disappearing; and only a few of the country houses survive without being on public view for tourists. Modern developments are often too numerous and too near to be seen easily in an historical perspective, but the recording of them is an important duty of the local historian.

Sites and buildings of historical interest

There are many visible remains of Oxfordshire's past in every village. This is a list of some of the best examples. It must not be assumed that all of them can be visited by the general public. This is especially true of private houses, but many of the others can be visited only at specified times. Places not open to the public are indicated by an asterisk. But in all cases students are asked to make every effort to respect the privacy of landowners: not to do so is often to imperil the work of subsequent researchers. Most archaeological features and public sites are under the protection of the Department of the Environment and scheduled under the Ancient Monuments Acts. Any disturbances of such sites is illegal and, in any case, is damaging to the interests of historians and the preservation of the past.

This is in no sense a gazetteer of sites and makes no pretence at completeness. The City and County Museum at Woodstock (see p. 62 below) is building up a complete record of sites, and students should consult this for details of sites, structures or buildings not mentioned or only briefly indicated here. Similarly, any information concerning a site, structure or building of any antiquity should be passed to the Museum. Its newsletter gives current information about the fate of sites and monuments and of research on them; and its leaflets, particularly those on motor trails, give information on the historical remains in many villages.

Some of the most interesting places for the historian are those where good examples of several buildings with different functions are preserved as a group such as the church, alms-houses and school at Ewelme; or those where there are visible remains from different periods on one spot. A good example of the latter is the deserted village site of Hampton Gay, bounded on one side by the ruins of an Elizabethan manor house burnt down in 1887 (see plate 2) and by the remains of a paper mill, and on the other side by the railway and the Oxford canal. Another is Blenheim Palace (1705–22) and its landscaped park at Woodstock, occupying the area of a medieval royal park in which the king's manor house stood, and in which both Grim's ditch and Akeman Street can be traced. Outside this park a medieval town was planned – a town whose regular shape has not been obscured by the many fine examples of later 17th-, 18th-, and 19th-century buildings which still meet the eye.

All the sites mentioned here are to be found on the Ordnance Survey map, and such a map, on the largest possible scale, is an indispensable tool to any working historian. In general, two of the best guides to the notable antiquities of Oxfordshire parishes are, on a small scale the Shell Guide of *Oxfordshire* by John Piper (1953) and on a larger scale the volumes of the *Victoria County History* (see p. 37 below).

PREHISTORIC

Evidence of prehistoric occupation survives in the Rollright stones and the Whispering Knights burial chamber at Rollright, the Hoar Stone at Enstone, Squires Clump round barrow at Sarsden and the long barrow at Lyneham. There are hill forts at Lyneham Camp, Knollbury in Chadlington,

Tadmarton Heath, Bozedown in Whitchurch and Dyke Hills at Dorchester with Sinodun Camp above it. One Grim's ditch is visible in Nuffield parish and another in Blenheim Park but there is some debate as to whether they are prehistoric or Anglo-Saxon. The Icknield Way along the Chilterns is visible, for example, near Watlington and Chinnor and is a trackway which was used in both prehistoric and later times.

ROMAN

At Alchester near Bicester the area of the walled town, now farmland, is clearly visible some four to six feet higher than the surrounding fields. At Dorchester the Roman town is for the most part below the present village, although the south-west corner of the wall and rampart is traceable as a low mound in the allotments. North Leigh villa is maintained by the Department of the Environment; one mosaic survives under cover. Widford church also contains the remains of a Roman domestic mosaic. The lines of the north–south Roman road through Dorchester and Alchester and of Akeman Street which also runs through Alchester can be seen in the lines of present roads, tracks and hedges. Akeman street can also be traced in Blenheim Park.

ANGLO-SAXON

The barrow at Asthall is of the 7th century. There is Anglo-Saxon work in several Oxfordshire churches, but the most extensive is in that at Langford where the Anglo-Saxon carvings include the famous figure of Christ crucified. Stuttles bank at Stratton Audley may be a Danish or a counter-Danish earthwork.

MEDIEVAL AND MODERN

Castles and fortifications. Earthworks of motte and bailey castles are visible at Ascott under Wychwood*, Chipping

Norton, Middleton Stoney and Swerford; other earthworks are at Deddington castle, at Stratton Audley and at Mixbury. There are 14th-century remains at Rotherfield Greys Court. The only surviving castles are late and much altered: Broughton (1306 and later), Shirburn* (1318 and later) and at Hanwell* (early 16th cent. – a very early use of brick). At Baynard's Green there was a 13th-century tournament ground.

Monasteries. The present parish church of Dorchester was the old abbey church, and the abbey guest house is now a museum which opens during the summer only. There are minor remains only of the alien priory at Cogges*, and other remains are at Goring church, Thame Park* and Wroxton Abbey*. Some ruins of Godstow Nunnery can be seen at Wolvercote.

Churches. Churches dating from medieval times are to be found in most of the county's towns and villages. Particularly fine examples are at Burford, Dorchester, Thame and Witney and, in the north of the county, in the three ironstone villages of Adderbury (see plate 1), Bloxham and Deddington. The outstanding example of Norman work is at Iffley, though such work is visible elsewhere, for example at Goring and Barford St. Michael. Fine examples of 15th-century architecture are at Ewelme and Minster Lovell, and of private chapels at Broughton castle (14th cent.) and at Rycote (16th cent., with Jacobean fittings).

Medieval wall-paintings can be seen at Chalgrove and Northmoor (14th cent.), North Leigh, South Leigh and North Stoke (15th cent.), Shorthampton (*c.* 1460) and elsewhere, and good examples of medieval stained glass at Kidlington (13th and 14th cents.), Chinnor (14th cent.), Shiplake (15th cent., from St. Omer) and Dorchester (13th and 14th cents.). Yarnton has some good 17th-century armorial glass. At Dorchester the sculpture of the windows, especially of the Jesse window, is remarkable. Dorchester is also one of the many churches with fine medieval brasses; there are other notable ones at Chipping

Norton, Chinnor, Thame, and Ewelme where a fine series runs from 1436 to 1606. Ewelme, Minister Lovell, Thame and Dorchester have examples of tombs of the 14th and 15th centuries. At North Leigh the Wilcote memorial of the 15th century combines both chapel and tomb.

Rood screens can be seen, amongst other places, at Stanton Harcourt (13th cent.), Broughton (14th cent., in stone), South Newington (14th cent.), Church Hanborough, Charlton on Otmoor and Somerton. A 14th-century stone reredos survives at Somerton.

Many churches contain fine alabaster and stone tombs and effigies dating from the 16th century onwards. Particularly noteworthy examples are at Burford and Rotherfield Greys; there is a good 16th-century canopied tomb at Waterperry and the Fettiplace effigies at Swinbrook are good examples of the 16th-century stonemason's art. Many places, Burford and Cropredy among them, have fine 'wool tombs' in the churchyards.

There are 18th-century churches at Banbury St. Mary (1797), Chislehampton (1763) and Nuneham Courtenay (1762), and 19th-century ones at Churchill (by Plowman), Leafield (by Scott), Wheatley (by Street) and Milton near Banbury (by Butterfield). There are many fine examples of Victorian stained glass, for example the William Morris glass at Bloxham. Distinguished nonconformist chapels may be seen, for instance at Adderbury (Quaker meeting house, 1675), Bicester (Congregational church, c. 1700), Charlbury (Quaker meeting house, 1779) and Cote (Baptist chapel, 17th cent., with additions); and Roman Catholic churches at Chipping Norton (1836) and Dorchester (1849). The Roman Catholic chapel at Stonor has been in continuous use since the later 13th century; Mapledurham House has a chapel dating from 1797.

Domestic buildings. Larger medieval houses can be seen either as ruins or incorporated into later houses at Cornbury Park*, Minister Lovell, Stonor and Stanton Harcourt*; and smaller houses at, for instance, Camoys Court at Stadhampton, and the Bird Cage Inn at Thame. R. B. Wood-Jones, *Traditional domestic architecture of the Banbury* *region* (1963) lists medieval incorporations into later structures in smaller properties in that area. Examples to notice are a medieval cellar in Hayes Shop, Chipping Norton, The Shaven Crown at Shipton under Wychwood and several houses in Deddington.

Moated sites of varying sizes can be easily picked out from the Ordnance Survey maps. Examples are, for instance, at Broughton Castle, Moorcourt at Lewknor, Beckley Park and Holton Park.

Oxfordshire possesses many fine examples of large post-medieval residences: from the 16th century Mapledurham, Rotherfield Greys Court and Kelmscott, the last of course with William Morris's additions; from the 17th century Pyrton, Chastleton, Cornbury Park, Rousham and Wroxton; from the 18th century Blenheim Palace, Ditchley, Nuneham Courtenay, Bletchingdon Park and Kirtlington Park; from the 19th century Friar Park at Henley, Kiddington Hall (*c.* 1850 by Barry), Wyfold Court near Checkendon (1872–6 by G. S. Clarke) and Shiplake Court (*c.* 1889–90 by George and Peto); and from the 20th century Middleton Park (by Lutyens) and Cornwell (by Clough Williams Ellis).

Many have landscaped gardens as at Rousham (W. Kent), Blenheim (Capability Brown), Nuneham Courtenay (W. Mason), Great Tew (J. Loudon) and Wroxton (S. Miller).

A walk round any large village and particularly round the market towns such as Burford, Chipping Norton, Woodstock, Henley or Witney will show many fine houses of all periods from the 16th to the 19th centuries.

Other buildings. Many buildings other than palaces, houses and churches afford great architectural and historical interest. Some types with a few examples are listed here:

Tithe barns: Church Enstone* and Adderbury* (14th cent.), Upper Heyford*, Swalcliffe* and Tadmarton* (15th cent.). Almshouses: Ewelme (15th cent.), Thame* (16th cent.), Chipping Norton*, Mapledurham, Kidlington, Charlbury 17th cent.), Witney* (near the church, 18th cent.), Deddington (1818), Glympton (1949). Market houses and town halls:

Burford (Tolsey, 15th cent.), Eynsham (17th cent.), Watling-ton (1664), Witney butter cross (1683), Woodstock (1766), Deddington (1806), Bampton (early Victorian). Inns: there are many of these from all periods; they are seen in their proper context on main coaching roads at places such as Tetsworth, Dorchester and Deddington. Schools: Ewelme (15th cent.), Somerton* (c. 1600), Burford (16th cent.), Bampton and Steeple Aston (17th cent.); 19th-century village schools are to be found in many villages often still in use. 19th-century workhouses: Chipping Norton*, Banbury*, Thame*, Witney*. Other buildings to watch out for are village lock-ups (e.g. at Wheatley), ice-houses (e.g. at Rycote), wells (e.g. at Stoke Row) and pumps, and dovecotes (e.g. at Minster Lovell).

Deserted villages and open fields. For a directory of deserted village sites see K. J. Allison, M. W. Beresford and J. G. Hurst, *The deserted villages of Oxfordshire* (1966): they range from the 12th-century village of Draitone or Treton in Bruern to the 16th-century village of Water Eaton. (See plate 8).

Remains of ridge and furrow can be seen in many parishes on clay soil for example at Water Eaton or Bicester, and especially in north Oxfordshire, for example at Shenington or South Newington.

Medieval planned towns. Several towns which grew up from an early attempt at deliberate planning, such as Banbury, Thame, Witney, and Woodstock, still retain evidence of the medieval plan.

Model villages. An 18th-century example is Nuneham Courte-nay, and the 19th century produced Great Tew, Churchill and Middleton Stoney as well as the Chartist village of Charterville in Minster Lovell.

Transport. The existence of the Thames has given the county many fine bridges. Examples are at Radcot and New-bridge (medieval), Shillingford, Swinford and Henley (18th cent.), Dorchester and Clifton Hampden (19th cent.). Swinford retains its tolls and has a contemporary toll-house. Toll-houses are found, too, on the old turnpike roads and some of these roads (the B.4437 from Charlbury to Woodstock, for example) have interesting milestones. The main canal in the county is that from Oxford to Birmingham: canal-side settlements can be discerned at Thrupp and Lower Heyford. The county was criss-crossed by the railways with their distinctive bridge and platform architecture: a pre-war edition of the Ordnance Survey map will indicate many which are now disused and abandoned. Good examples of station architecture are at Kingham and Charlbury.

Industry. The county's main industries centring on cloth and stone have left their remains. The blanket and cloth mills of Witney and the Windrush valley can still be seen. Bliss's Tweed Mills* at Chipping Norton is a splendid structure from 1872. Waterpower was used for paper mills at Wolvercote and Sandford (still active) and at Hampton Gay and Eynsham (remains only; see plate 3). Windmills remain at Bloxham, Great Haseley, Wheatley and North Leigh, and watermills in the river valleys as at Mapledurham, Clifton in Deddington and Cuddesdon. Quarries existed in numerous places, the most famous at Stonesfield, Taynton, Burford and Bladon. There were ochre pits at Wheatley. The local industry of gloving in the Woodstock area left few remains though the factories there and at Charlbury are sometimes now private houses. Banbury and to a lesser extent Witney and Henley were the only places which were greatly affected by industrial development in the 19th century.

II

Sources and Repositories of Oxfordshire History

Notes on general reading for local historians

There is one national historical periodical which deals exclusively with the field of local history. This is *The Local Historian*, the quarterly journal of the Standing Conference for Local History. It began publication in 1952 under the title *The Amateur Historian* and changed its name in 1968. Some articles of lasting value from early numbers now out of print have been re-issued in pamphlet form. These include, for example: J. Thirsk, *Sources of information on population 1500–1760* (1965) and M. W. Beresford, *The unprinted census returns of 1841, 1851, and 1861 for England and Wales* (1966). Current numbers serve a very useful purpose in keeping local historians in touch with comparable work done in other counties and in suggesting new subjects for inquiry and new angles of approach in local studies. They also make it possible to keep abreast of the ever-increasing output of publications in this field. Orders and inquiries about subscriptions should be made to the National Council of Social Service (Subscriptions Dept. L.H.), 26 Bedford Square, London, WC1B 3HU.

The Historical Association publishes its journal *History* three times a year. Since 1962 it has included a valuable series called *Short Guides to Records,* each of which prints an example of a different type of record with information about where such records can be found and what use can be made of them; examples are *Wills* (1965) by R. Sharpe France and *Enclosure awards and acts* (1966) by W. E. Tate. All 25 leaflets are shortly to appear in book form. The Historical Association also publishes many pamphlets of value to the local historian. These include F. W. Kuhlicke and F. G. Emmison, *English local history handlist* (1965); F. G. Emmison and I. Gray, *County Records* (1967); F. G. Emmison, *How to read local archives 1550–1700* (1971); K. C. Newton, *Medieval local records: a reading aid* (1971); and J. Youings, *Local record sources in print and in progress 1971– 72* (1972). Full lists of publications can be obtained on application to The Secretary, The Historical Association, 59a Kennington Park Road, London, SE11 4JH.

The following books are recommended for general reading:

W. G. Hoskins, *Local history in England* (2nd edition, 1972)
W. B. Stephens, *Sources for English local history* (1973)
R. B. Pugh, *How to write a parish history* (1954)
W. E. Tate, *The parish chest* (3rd edition, 1969)
John West, *Village records* (1962)

The following will be found to be helpful to anyone using early documentary material:

H. E. P. Grieve, *Examples of English handwriting* (1954)
E. A. Gooder, *Latin for local history, an introduction* (1961)
Julian Cornwall, *How to read old title deeds XVI–XIX centuries* (2nd impression, 1970)
C. T. Martin, *The record interpreter* (re-issue, 1949)
C. R. Cheney, *Handbook of dates for students of English history* (reprint, 1955)

Oxfordshire Printed Material

1. SOME EARLY BOOKS ABOUT OXFORDSHIRE

Most English counties have classical histories written by antiquarians of the 17th to 19th centuries. William Dugdale's *Antiquities of Warwickshire* (1656) or John Nichol's *History and antiquities of the county of Leicester* (1795–1815) are examples of works which still provide the indispensable foundations of local history studies in their counties. Oxfordshire is one of the less fortunate counties with no basic work of comparable stature. Descriptions of Oxfordshire can, of course, be found in antiquarian works of a general character, such as William Camden's *Britannia* first published in Latin in 1586; but Oxford itself, 'the English Athens', was the natural focus of attention. In the same way later travellers were so dazzled by the beauties of Oxford that they were often blind to the less spectacular interest of the surrounding countryside. The earliest book wholly devoted to the county is *The natural history of Oxfordshire* (1677) by Dr. Robert Plot, first keeper of the Ashmolean Museum and Professor of Chemistry. Plot's work is of unusual interest but, as its name implies, it is mainly concerned with natural resources and phenomena, and any historical information to be found in it is incidental.

In 1695, White Kennett, then vicar of Ambrosden and later Bishop of Peterborough, published *Parochial antiquities attempted in the history of Ambrosden, Burcester, and other adjacent parts in the counties of Oxford and Bucks.*, which may claim to be the first in any county of the long line of parish histories written by learned clergymen of antiquarian tastes. The historian John Dunkin, born in Bicester, knew the same countryside well; his *History and antiquities of Bicester* appeared in 1816. He collected materials with the intention of writing an account of the whole county which would have removed the reproach that Oxfordshire had no history. But only one part was completed: *The history and antiquities of the hundreds of Bullingdon and Ploughley* (1823). Dunkin's work was adversely criticized in the *Gentleman's Magazine* for devoting too much attention to the common man and displaying anti-establishment tendencies, characteristics which may make the modern reader regret the more that the work was never finished. His unpublished collections belong to the Guildhall Library, London, but they are now deposited in the Bodleian. Two other works of the same period may be mentioned: Arthur Young's *View of the agriculture of Oxford* (1809) and Skelton's *Engraved illustrations of the principal antiquities of Oxfordshire* (1823).

2. GENERAL BIBLIOGRAPHY OF THE COUNTY

The publication of *A Bibliography of printed works relating to Oxfordshire* (*excluding the University and City of Oxford*), by E. H. Cordeaux and D. H. Merry in 1955 makes it unnecessary to attempt a comprehensive reading list in this handbook. The *Bibliography* is an invaluable work of reference, listing all the printed material relating to Oxfordshire in the Bodleian Library: for the convenience of Bodleian readers, the shelfmarks are given. The more general material is arranged under subject headings (for example, Economic history: communications) while material relating to a particular locality is listed under the names of towns and villages. The *Bibliography* is much more than a list of books; articles of Oxfordshire interest which have appeared in national periodicals, from the *Gentleman's Magazine* to the *Economic History Review*, are included as well as articles in Oxfordshire periodicals. References are given to printed acts of parliament concerned with such subjects as enclosures and turnpikes, and to ephemeral printed matter such as sale catalogues, rarely preserved and hard to trace. No bibliography, however excellent, can long remain complete and it is now nearly twenty years since this one appeared. The intention was to keep 'Cordeaux and Merry' up to date by publishing frequent supplements. In fact only one supplement has been printed, adding books published up to the end of 1956 with some additions and corrections to the original entries. This supplement is to be found, in two parts, in volume VI of *The Bodleian Library Record*. More recent accessions have been noted in an interleaved copy of 'Cordeaux and Merry' which is available in Duke Humfrey's Reading Room in the Bodleian. Another way of keeping in touch with publications which have appeared since 1957 is to consult the lists of recent books and articles given at the end of volumes of *Oxoniensia* (see p. 39 below). These notices include references to articles of local interest which have appeared in national periodicals, such as *Archaeologia*.

Much of the valuable work accomplished in archaeological and historical studies since 1957 is to be found in articles in *Oxoniensia*, in the editions of documentary materials published by the local record societies and in the recent volumes of the *Victoria County History*. The following is a short list of some recommended books which have appeared as separate publications in the last fifteen years:

E. Goshawk, *Fifield Merrymouth* (1957)

W. Potts, *A history of Banbury* (1958)

J. H. Baker, *The Ipsden country* (1959)

D. McClatchey, *Oxfordshire clergy 1777–1869* (1960)

M. G. Hobson and K. L. H. Price, *Otmoor and its seven towns* (1961)

H. M. Colvin, *A history of Deddington* (1962)

R. B. Wood-Jones, *Traditional domestic architecture of the Banbury region* (1963)

A. M. Taylor, *Gilletts, bankers at Banbury and Oxford* (1964)

P. D. A. Harvey, *A medieval Oxfordshire village: Cuxham 1240–1460* (1965)

K. J. Allison, M. W. Beresford and J. G. Hurst, *The deserted villages of Oxfordshire* (1966)

R. E. Moreau, *The departed village: Berrick Salome at the turn of the century* (1968)

A. S. T. Fisher, *The history of Broadwell . . . . with Filkins, Kelmscott & Holywell* (1968); *The history of Kencot* (1970); *The history of Westwell* (1972)

C. Ponsonby, *Wootton: the anatomy of an Oxfordshire village, 1945–1968* (1968)

A. Plummer and R. E. Early, *The blanket makers 1669–1969. A history of Charles Early and Marriott (Witney) Ltd.* (1969)

P. D. A. Harvey, *Banbury* in *Historic Towns*, ed. M. D. Lobel, volume I (1969)

1. A drawing made in 1822 by J. C. Buckler of the Elizabethan manor house of Hampton Gay, burnt down in 1887 and now in ruins. (*Bodleian Library, MS. Top. Oxon. a. 67, no. 289*).

2. A drawing by J. C. Buckler of Adderbury church from the north east, 1825. (*Bodleian Library, MS. Top. Oxon. a. 65, no. 29*).

3. A Buckler drawing made in 1824 of the paper mill at Eynsham. The mill no longer exists. (*Bodleian Library, MS. Top. Oxon. a. 66, no. 254*).

4. The first entries on a court roll of the manor of Beckley and Horton, 1 October 1657. Like all legal documents of the Commonwealth period this is in English, but court rolls are usually in Latin until 1733. (*Bodleian Library, MS. Rolls Oxon. 164*).

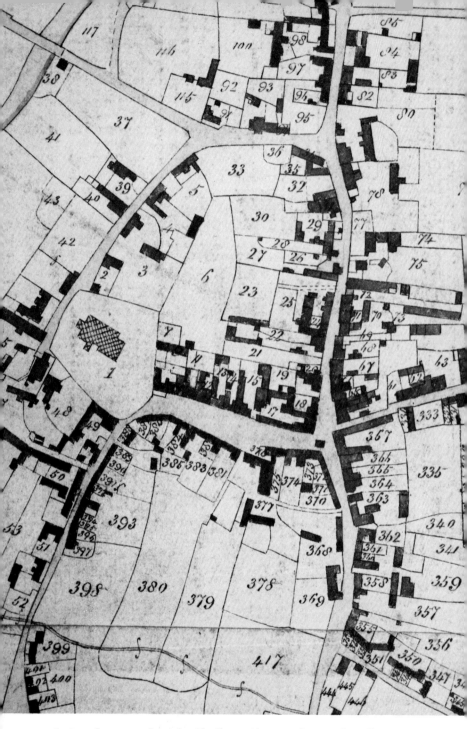

5. An enlargement from the Charlbury tithe map showing the village centre in 1848. (*Bodleian Library*).

LANDOWNERS.	OCCUPIERS.	Numbers referring to the Plan.	NAME AND DESCRIPTION of LANDS AND PREMISES.	STATE of CULTIVATION.	QUANTITIES in STATUTE MEASURE.			PAYABLE TO Vicar			PAYA to Haile
John —— stinned,	Richard Tidmarsh	355	Tenement and Garden			.	7	.	.	.	
s. John ——	John. Padbury	175	Eight Leys	Pasture	4	3	17	1	5	6	
		176	Badgers Close	Meadow	2	.	18	.	10	10	
		177	Eight Leys	do	1	3	7	.	9	7	
		178	Eight Leys	do	2	2	10	.	12	11	
					11	1	12	2	18	10	.
s. Rebecca ——	Thomas Kibble	332	Tenement			.	3	.	.	.	
	William. Compton	384	Tenement and Garden			.	10	.	.	.	
	Herself	364	Tenement and Garden			.	17	.	.	.	
	Tho.ˢ Padbury	113	Near Baywell Turnpike	Arable	4	2	4	.	7	2	1
ser. John ——	John. Hinch	397	Tenement and Garden			.	9	.	.	.	
ld. Thomas ——	John. Webb & another	346	Two Tenements and Gardens			.	17	.	.	.	
		347	Methodist Meeting house			.	10	.	.	.	
Mary ——	Tho.ˢ Gomm & another	440	Two Tenements & Gardens			.	18	.	.	.	
. William ——	Himself	10	House. Outbuildings and Garden			.	11	.	.	.	
		322	Tenement			.	3	.	.	.	
						.	14	.	.	.	.
John ——	Himself	443	Tenement and Garden			.	17	.	.	.	
Henry and ney. Charles	Edward Cross	98	Dog Public House, Yard and Garden			.	33	.	.	.	
s Thomas ——	Himself	31	House and Yard			.	6	.	.	.	
. Abel and y William	Richard. Barrett and another	401	Two Tenements & Garden			.	6	.	.	.	

6. Page 8 of the Charlbury tithe award which lists some of the properties shown on the map opposite. (*Bodleian Library*).

7. A page from Mapledurham churchwardens' accounts showing payments made for 'Beautyfieing the Church' and a rate collected for the purpose, 1737. (Bodleian Library, MS. D.D. Par. Mapledurham e.1, fols. 45ᵛ–46ʳ).

A Rate for Beautyfieing the Church of Mapledurham in the County of Oxon: Made by John Lewington &c as Rich Collier Church Wardens 1737 at 2 halfpenny in the Pound

	£	s	d
Thomas Brigham Esq.ʳ	8	4	2
Rich Collier for Gile	2	1	3
Rich Collier for Lock form	0	4	5
Rich Collier malt house	0	3	9
Rich Collier the mower	0	1	0
Rich Collier Bevors	1	5	0
John Lewington Chaze farm	0	5	2
W.ᵐ Allnwright Fairey	0	9	0
Edw.ᵈ Battler Sen.ʳ for Pit house	0	16	10
Rich Allnwright Bottom form	0	4	2
Edw.ᵈ Battler Sen.ʳ Greenah Green	0	1	5
Rich.ᵈ Biddle for his form	0	0	2
Rich.ᵈ Biddle for Taylors	1	11	3
Rich Biddle Mecrow	0	5	0
Rich Allnway new form &c	0	8	6
Edw.ᵈ Freeman Ship ways	0	2	1
Edw.ᵈ Battler Red woods	0	2	9
Abraham Crofwell Jun.ʳ Ends			
Edw.ᵈ Battler Wisers			

The Expence of Beautyfieing y Church Don in y year 1737.

The Particulars.

	£	s	d
Paid Will. Collier 10=10= 0 as it was agreed at the vestry for new Plastering the Body of y Church Frosting the old off and writeing the Lords Prayer the Comandmts the Crede Containing 2000 Letters at a half Penny a Letter: the Plastering at 8.¹ p.ʳ yorᵈ Containing 250 yards	10	10	0
Paid him for Painting y Beams of y Church, one for writeing the names of the Benefactors to y Poor	0	10	0
Paid to Will. Collier in all	11	0	0
Paid Daniel Wells a Bill for White-washing and Plastering y Little Church, y Church Sealing, y Gallery Seeling and Bellfree &c. Containing 405 yords at 2½.ᵈ yord	03	7	6
Paid him for mending y Church short wall work mensins &c. Stuff	00	2	6

8. An aerial photograph of the site of Nether Chalford in Enstone, a medieval deserted village. (*Cambridge University Collection of Aerial Photographs, LU 10; copyright reserved*).

9. A photograph by Henry Taunt of the sheep fair at Thame in 1897. (Oxford City Libraries, Taunt Collection).

M. Toynbee and P. Young, *Cropredy Bridge, 1644. The campaign and the battle* (1970)

B. Reaney, *The class struggle in 19th century Oxfordshire: the social and communal background to the Otmoor disturbances of 1830 to 1835* (History Workshop Pamphlets no. 3, 1970)

G. H. Dannatt, *The Oxfordshire election of 1754* (Oxfordshire County Council Record Publication no. 6, 1970)

3. THE VICTORIA COUNTY HISTORY

The *Victoria History* of the counties of England is a large national project which was begun at the very end of the 19th century. Work on Oxfordshire is still in progress. Volumes 1 and 2 were published in 1899 and 1907. Volume 1 contains a complete translation of the Domesday survey for the county. The general articles in volume 2 are still of value, especially Dr. H. E. Salter's contributions on ecclesiastical history and the religious houses. Volume 3 is devoted entirely to the University and volume 4 (not yet published) will cover the city of Oxford. The remaining volumes will contain brief histories of every parish in the county, arranged alphabetically under hundreds. The following have appeared to date:

Volume 5 (1957). *Bullingdon Hundred*: Albury (with Tiddington), Ambrosden, Marsh Baldon, Toot Baldon, Beckley, Cowley, Cuddesdon (with Wheatley), Elsfield, Forest Hill, Garsington, Headington, Holton, Horspath, Iffley, Littlemore, Marston, Merton, Nuneham Courtenay, Piddington, St. Clements, Sandford on Thames, Shotover, Stanton St. John, Stowood, Waterperry, Woodeaton.

Volume 6 (1959). *Ploughley Hundred*: Ardley, Bicester, Bletchingdon, Bucknell, Charlton on Otmoor, Chesterton, Cottisford, Finmere, Fringford, Fritwell, Godington, Hampton Gay, Hampton Poyle, Hardwick, Hethe, Lower

D

Heyford, Upper Heyford, Islip, Kirtlington, Launton, Middleton Stoney, Mixbury, Newton Purcell, Noke, Oddington, Shelswell, Somerton, Souldern, Stoke Lyne, Stratton Audley, Tusmore, Wendlebury, Weston on the Green.

Volume 7 (1962). *Dorchester and Thame Hundreds. Dorchester*: Chislehampton, Clifton Hampden, Culham, Dorchester (with Burcot), Drayton St. Leonard, Stadhampton, South Stoke. *Thame*: Great Milton, Tetsworth, Thame, Waterstock.

Volume 8 (1964). *Lewknor and Pyrton Hundreds. Lewknor*: Adwell, Aston Rowant, Britwell Salome, Chinnor, Crowell, Emmington, Lewknor, Sydenham. *Pyrton*: Pishill, Pyrton, Stoke Talmage, Watlington, South Weston, Wheatfield.

Volume 9 (1969). *Bloxham Hundred*: Adderbury, Alkerton, Bloxham, Broughton, Drayton, Hanwell, Horley and Hornton, Shenington, Tadmarton, Wigginton, Wroxton.

Volume 10 (1972). *Banbury Hundred*: Banbury, Charlbury, Cropredy (with Great and Little Bourton, Claydon, Clattercote, Mollington, Prescote and Wardington), Swalcliffe.

Anyone wishing to study his own parish history should first see whether it has yet been the subject of a V.C.H. article. If it has, he will find much of the basic hard work done for him and in the footnotes he will find full reference to the sources available both in print and in manuscript. But the V.C.H. articles, valuable as they are, should be regarded as a beginning rather than an end; most local historians with first-hand knowledge of the locality and its people will be able to make substantial additions, especially in the modern period.

The arrangement of the V.C.H. articles is also intended to help readers interested in a particular subject over a wider area than the single parish. Many aspects of local history can be studied with greater interest and profit on a comparative basis: enclosure, poor relief, and education are obvious examples. The history of the great estates, of transport, marketing or wages can only be pursued on this wider scale.

4. LOCAL PERIODICALS

Publications of the Oxfordshire Architectural and Historical Society. The Oxford Architectural and Historical Society (as it was known until 1972) is the oldest publishing society in the county. It was founded in 1839 as 'the Oxford Society for promoting the study of Gothic Architecture' and it was only in 1860 that its scope was widened to include history and archaeology. Its early *Proceedings* (1839–1901) contain some papers of importance, for example, C. H. Firth's 'Chronological summary of the Civil War in Oxfordshire, Buckinghamshire and Berkshire' (new series, vol. 5, 1900). Its journal, *Oxoniensia*, which appears annually was begun in 1936 to enable scholars to publish articles on the archaeology, history and architecture of Oxford and its neighbourhood, to report on recent finds, and to review books of local interest.

The Oxfordshire Archaeological Society was founded in 1852 as the Archaeological Society of North Oxfordshire. Its title was expanded to the Archaeological and Natural History Society of North Oxfordshire in 1856, but a more important change occurred in 1887 when the Society resolved that its activities should cover the whole county and so changed its name to the Oxfordshire Archaeological Society. It published *Reports* and *Transactions* continuously until 1972 when it was amalgamated with the Oxford Architectural and Historical Society described above to form the Oxfordshire Architectural and Historical Society. From 1958 the Archaeological Society also published (at first jointly with the Oxfordshire Rural Community Council) a bulletin known as *Top. Oxon.: Oxfordshire Local History.* This periodical has been subject to many vicissitudes but it is now appearing annually as another publication of the newly amalgamated Oxfordshire Architectural and Historical Society. It serves a useful purpose in providing an opportunity for publishing shorter articles, and notes and news.

Both *Oxoniensia* and *Top. Oxon.* are available to members of the amalgamated society for varying rates of subscription. Intending subscribers should apply to the Honorary Treasurer of the Society, Ashmolean Museum, Oxford. *Top. Oxon.* is also available to non-members who should apply to one of the editors: Miss S. Barnes, County Record Office, or Mr. Malcolm Graham, Oxford City Libraries.

The Oxford Historical Society. The Oxford Historical Society was founded in 1884 as a memorial to the historian John Richard Green who was a native of Oxford and had planned such a society before his death in 1883. Its object was and is to publish historical records of the University and City of Oxford. Many of these records, however, extend well beyond the limits of Oxford itself and provide essential material for the county. Obvious examples are the cartularies of the great religious houses: St. Frideswide, volumes I and II (1895–6); Eynsham, volumes I and II (1907–8); and Oseney, volumes IV and V concerned with properties outside Oxford (1934–5). The notebooks of Oxford antiquaries are also important for historians working on Oxfordshire subjects: notably, *The life and times of Anthony Wood,* published in five volumes (1891–1900), and *Remarks and collections of Thomas Hearne,* in eleven volumes (1885–1921). Publications in this series are separately listed in 'Cordeaux and Merry' under their appropriate places or subject headings. The complete list to 1957 can conveniently be seen in E. L. C. Mullins, *Texts and calendars,* one of the Royal Historical Society's handbooks (1958), pp. 412–13.

Anyone wishing to become a subscriber should apply to the Honorary Treasurer: Mr. J. P. Wells, Oxford City Libraries, Westgate, Oxford.

The Oxfordshire Record Society. The Oxfordshire Record

Society was founded in 1919 with the object of printing documents relating to the history of the county. It thus comple-
ments the work of the Oxford Historical Society. The Record
Society has also published cartularies, for the priories of
Sandford (vols. 19, 22, 1937, 1941) and Thame (vols. 25–6,
1947–8), and parochial collections of the antiquaries, Anthony
Wood and Richard Rawlinson (vols. 2, 4, 11, 1920–9). Other
classes of records included in the series are chantry certificates (vol. 1, 1919), churchwardens' presentments (vol. 10,
1928), hearth tax returns of 1665 (vol. 21, 1940), protestation
returns of 1641–2 (vol. 36, 1955), early wills (vol. 39, 1958)
and probate inventories (vol. 44, 1965), clergy visitation
answers of 1738 (vol. 38, 1957) and 1854 (vol. 35, 1954) and
Henley borough records (vol. 41, 1960). A full list of these
publications to 1957 can also be seen in Mullins, *Texts and
calendars,* pp. 408–11. The Society has provisionally accepted
for future publication a number of other interesting and
useful texts.

An annual subscription entitles members to receive
volumes at less than the price at which they are sold to the
public and to attend annual general meetings. Applications
for membership should be sent to the Honorary Treasurer,
Bodleian Library, Oxford.

The Banbury Historical Society. The Banbury Historical
Society was founded in 1957 to encourage interest in the
history of the town of Banbury and neighbouring parts of
Oxfordshire, Northamptonshire and Warwickshire. Its
regular publications are the magazine *Cake and Cockhorse*
issued quarterly to members and its annual *Records Series*
begun in 1959, which has already made a significant contribution to the printed record material available to Oxfordshire
historians. The series includes parish registers, churchwardens' accounts and constables' books, an index of
Banbury wills and inventories and a volume on clockmaking
in Oxfordshire 1400–1850. Other occasional publications
have included *Old Banbury – a short popular history,* by
E. R. C. Brinkworth. Applications for membership should

be sent to the Honorary Secretary, Miss C. G. Bloxham, Banbury Museum.

5.   LOCAL NEWSPAPERS

A complete list of local newspapers is given in 'Cordeaux and Merry', pp. 141–5. The oldest and most important of these is *Jackson's Oxford Journal* begun in 1753, continued as the *Oxford Journal Illustrated* from 1909 and incorporated in the *Oxford Times* in 1928. Banbury, Bicester, Chipping Norton, Henley, Thame and Witney have all had their own papers, all (except that of Chipping Norton) begun around the middle of the 19th century and some of them still running.

Local papers are a valuable source for the historian working in modern periods. Although the space devoted to local news tends to be meagre in the 18th-century issues, the proportion of local to national news reported increases steadily. Much material of interest is to be found in the advertisements. The greatest deterrent for historians wanting to make use of information in local newspapers lies in the absence of indexes. For the researcher interested in a single event which he is able to date, no difficulty arises. But it can be a very slow and laborious task to work through a long run of papers in the hope of finding references to a place or a subject of continuing interest. Fortunately, however, an excellent index has now been compiled by Miss E. C. Davies for the years 1753–1780 of *Jackson's Oxford Journal*; copies are available in the Bodleian, the County Record Office and the City Library, all of which have sets of the *Journal*. Work is now in progress on a continuation of the index to 1800, and it is much to be hoped that it will later extend to the 19th century. The only place which has complete runs of all the Oxfordshire local newspapers is the British Museum's Newspaper Library, Colindale Avenue, London NW9 5HE, but many are also available at the Bodleian Library, the County Record Office, the City Library and the newspapers' own offices.

While the value of local papers to the historian lies

primarily in their reports of contemporary events and contemporary comment upon them, it should be noted that most of these papers from time to time print articles of a historical nature. Some of these have been contributed by reliable scholars and some have incorporated memories and traditions which would otherwise have been lost.

Libraries and Record Repositories

It is always advisable for the student to write to a library or record repository in advance of a visit providing as many details as possible of his requirements and of his topic of research. This gives the librarian or archivist an opportunity to devote some thought to the problem and thus saves the student's time on arrival; and it often prevents a fruitless visit.

1.   OXFORDSHIRE COUNTY LIBRARY

Address and access: Oxfordshire County Library, Holton Park, Wheatley, Oxford, OX9 1QQ. Tel. Wheatley 2234. Open: 9.0 a.m. to 5.0 p.m. on Mondays, Tuesdays, Thursdays and Fridays; 9.0 a.m. to 7.15 p.m. on Wednesdays.

The County Library has a fine collection of printed material for Oxfordshire history. Most of the books mentioned in the previous section and many more will be found there; fuller reading lists are available on application to the Librarian. With the exception of certain rare and valuable books, and some works of reference, all the books can be borrowed direct from the headquarters of the Library or through the branch libraries and travelling van service. There are branch libraries at Adderbury, Bampton, Benson, Bicester, Burford, Carterton, Charlbury, Chinnor, Chipping Norton, Deddington, Eynsham, Goring, Henley, Hook Norton, Horspath, Kidlington, Littlemore, Old Marston, Risinghurst, Sandhills, Sonning Common, Stonesfield, Thame, Watlington, Wheatley, Witney, Woodstock and Wychwood.

There are travelling vans serving central, east, north, south, south-west and west Oxfordshire based respectively on headquarters, Bicester, Deddington, Watlington, Witney and Wychwood.

In addition to its collections of printed books on local history, the County Library has some unprinted source materials; some village scrapbooks and similar materials have been deposited there. Application should be made to the Librarian for permission to see such material at Holton Park, where advice and information about local history is readily given.

2. OXFORD CITY LIBRARIES: LOCAL HISTORY COLLECTION AND CITY ARCHIVES

Address and access: Oxford City Libraries, Westgate Oxford, OX1 1DJ. Tel. Oxford 41717. Open: 9.15 a.m. to 8.0 p.m. on Mondays to Wednesdays and Fridays; 9.15 a.m. to 5.0 p.m. on Thursdays and Saturdays. Persons wishing to consult city archives are advised to give advance notice as many of these are housed in the Town Hall in St. Aldate's. Xerox copying is available.

The City Library has a good collection of printed books relating to the county as well as to the city. This includes early maps and directories, *Jackson's Oxford Journal* and other early newspapers. Apart from printed materials, it has two valuable sources not available elsewhere. The first is the Henry Taunt collection of historic photographs of Oxford and the surrounding country covering the period from 1860 to 1920 (see plate 9). A recent admirable introduction to this collection including many reproductions of photographs is Malcolm Graham's *Henry Taunt of Oxford: a Victorian photographer* (1973). The second is a complete set of microfilm copies of the enumerators' books for the Oxfordshire census returns of 1841, 1851, 1861 and 1871. The returns are important sources for tracing the history of individual families. They can also profitably be used as a basis for a social survey of the local community in the nineteenth century.

Most of the city archives relate of course to the history of Oxford, but this collection includes some deeds of properties outside Oxford, notably in the parishes of Bletchingdon, Eynsham, Garsington, Haseley and Sandford on Thames. Most of these relate to properties belonging to Oxford city charities. Under the Oxford Extension Act of 1928 the city acquired the parish council records of the villages on the outskirts of Oxford which became part of the city in that year, that is Cowley, Iffley, Headington and Wolvercote. The city records also include minute books of the Headington Board of Guardians from 1841 to 1927.

3. BANBURY PUBLIC LIBRARY

Address and access: Banbury Public Library, Marlborough Rd., Banbury, Oxon., OX16 8DF. Tel Banbury 2282. Open: 9.30 a.m. to 7.0 p.m. on Mondays and Wednesdays to Fridays; 9.30 a.m. to 1.0 p.m. on Tuesdays; 9.30 a.m. to 5.0 p.m. on Saturdays.

The borough of Banbury is the only other local authority in the county which at present provides a library and museum service. Its Public Library opened in 1948 and took over the library of the Banbury Mechanics' Institute which had been founded in 1835. It has a considerable stock of printed material relating to Banbury and district including Banbury directories, miscellanea collected by the Unitarian printer, William Potts, and a further collection of local printed ephemera arranged by subjects. Another valuable source for the history of Banbury and district is an extra-illustrated copy of Alfred Beesley's *History of Banbury* (1841). Some original Banbury records are also deposited in the Library including minute books of the Mechanics' Institute. Banbury parish records are deposited partly here and partly in the Bodleian; a list showing which each library holds is in *Cake and Cockhorse*, volume 2, no. 9 (1964), pp. 154–6. The Library has runs of *The Banbury Guardian* and *The Banbury Advertiser* from 1948 only.

4. THE BODLEIAN LIBRARY

Address and access: The Bodleian Library, Oxford, OX1 3BG. Tel. Oxford 44675. Open: 9.0 a.m. to 10.0 p.m. on Mondays to Fridays during University terms, 9.0 a.m. to 7.0 p.m. in vacations; 9.0 a.m. to 1.0 p.m. on all Saturdays. Closed: Good Friday to Easter Monday, the day of Encaenia (usually the last Wednesday in June), the week beginning with the Summer Bank Holiday, and 24–31 December. A reader's ticket is required, a form of application for which is obtainable from the Library. Schoolchildren cannot be admitted as readers. There is normally about an hour's wait for material housed in the bookstack so it is advisable to order such books and manuscripts in advance by post or phone. Xerox copies, photostats, photographs and microfilms can be supplied, and order forms giving details of these services are obtainable from the Library.

The Bodleian is the library of the University of Oxford named after Sir Thomas Bodley who refounded it between 1598 and 1602. It has been accumulating books and manuscripts for more than three and a half centuries, and is now a large institution with a variety of functions, housed in several buildings. It is not a lending library, and all books must be read in the Library. Its mere size and the wealth of its collections are apt to prove bewildering to newcomers. Students of local history using the Library for the first time should go to Duke Humfrey's Reading Room in the Old Library, where many topographical reference books are on open shelves. Manuscripts and documents have to be read in this reading room, and all the catalogues and indexes of such material are housed there. In the Bodleian it is not possible to look in a single index to find what there is relating to a particular parish or subject. There are at least six types of material in the Library which are important for Oxfordshire

history, each with different finding aids. These classes of
material are briefly described below; further details of the
finding aids are given in a leaflet obtainable from the Department of Western Manuscripts.

1. *Printed materials.* As one of the national copyright libraries
the Bodleian receives copies of all new books and periodicals
published in this country, and so its holdings include almost
all the printed material Oxfordshire historians need to
consult. This includes a number of early or rare books and
pamphlets not available elsewhere in the county, good collections of poll books and county directories, and a complete
run of *Jackson's Oxford Journal.* As 'Cordeaux and Merry'
(see p. 35 above) gives the Bodleian shelfmark of all the
books it lists, most Oxfordshire printed material not on open
shelves can be ordered from the bookstack by quoting shelfmarks from this work.

2. *Topographical manuscripts.* The Bodleian's general collections of western manuscripts include many papers of
Oxfordshire antiquaries acquired by gift or purchase from
the 17th century onwards. Some of the most notable of these
are the collections of Anthony Wood (1632–95), Richard
Rawlinson (1690–1755), Richard Gough (1735–1809), Henry
Hinton (1749–1816), W. H. Turner (1833–80), Percy Man-
ning (1870–1917), Canon W. J. Oldfield (1857–1934) and the
Rev. H. E. Salter (1863–1951). Their papers consist in part
of the antiquaries' own notes and comments and copies of
records and of monumental inscriptions. Bodleian topographical collections also include a wide variety of original
documents and manuscripts relating to the history of the
county, many of them collected by these antiquaries, and
ranging from a 13th-century cartulary of Sandford Priory
bought from Wood to 19th-century rate books for Shirburn,
his own parish, given by Salter. From 1884 onwards most
of this material has been referenced 'MSS. Top. Oxon.'.
 All topographical manuscripts acquired by the Bodleian up
to 1915 are catalogued and indexed in the Library's two

printed sets of catalogues of western manuscripts. Most Oxfordshire manuscripts of this kind acquired since 1915 are catalogued and indexed in P. S. Spokes, *Summary catalogue of manuscripts ... relating to the city, county and University of Oxford Accessions from 1916 to 1962* (1964). This catalogue shows very well how varied and miscellaneous are the contents of 'MSS. Top. Oxon.'.

3. *Local records.* The manuscripts described above are the Bodleian's own property. The Library also now holds on deposit many collections of Oxfordshire archives, most of which have only come into the Library since the last war. The first big acquisition of local records was however made in 1878, long before librarians and archivists thought in terms of 'revocable deposit'. In that year the Oxford and Berkshire archdeaconry records, both housed in one archidiaconal registry near Folly Bridge in Oxford 'were put at the disposal of the Bodleian Curators', and these are listed in the *Summary catalogue of western manuscripts in the Bodleian Library,* vol. 5, pp. 157–84, nos. 25579–26120.

In 1915 and 1947 most of the Oxford diocesan records, dating from the foundation of the see in 1542, were transferred to the Library from the diocesan registry. Since 1947 there have been further transfers of recent diocesan records, and of the bishops' less formal records which had been kept at Cuddesdon Palace; and the records of the bishops' estates have been transferred to the Library by the Church Commissioners. These diocesan records are listed by class of document in typescript.

Canon W. J. Oldfield compiled a parochial index of many of the archdeaconry and diocesan records and of some of the topographical manuscripts mentioned above, and further references have been added to his index. Oldfield also compiled a separate parish index of the diocesan papers previously at Cuddesdon. Anyone wishing to use these records for parish history should begin by consulting these 'Oldfields', where for instance glebe terriers, faculties and consecrations, mortgages to alter parsonage houses, certificates of dissenting meeting houses, returns of schools and diocesan correspondence are all listed by parishes. The Oxford diocesan records are exceptionally rich in sets of clergy's answers to printed visitation queries from 1738 onwards, which are mentioned above (p. 22) as a particularly valuable source for church and parish history. The diocesan records are also our main source of information about Oxfordshire parish clergy. Another index by Canon Oldfield, known as his 'Clerus', lists all references to clergy in the bishops' registers of institutions and ordinations, both by persons and parishes.

The Bodleian now also houses the probate records of the courts of the bishop and archdeacon of Oxford and of the officials of 'peculiars' exempt from the bishop's jurisdiction. These records of Oxfordshire wills and administrations extend from the early 16th century to 1857. During the period from about 1580 to about 1720 they also include many probate inventories listing the deceased person's goods, sometimes room by room. There are manuscript person indexes of all these probate records, but no place indexes. Anyone wishing to find the surviving inventories for a particular parish needs to know the surnames of the main families living there in the 17th century, so that he can look for these in the person indexes.

In 1951 the Bishop of Oxford named the Bodleian as the repository where Oxfordshire incumbents might deposit their parish records if they so wished. The Library now holds some or all of the records of about one hundred parishes. Besides registers of baptisms, marriages and burials, some of these include vestry minutes, churchwardens', overseers', constables' and surveyors' accounts, records of parish charities and papers relating to the administration of the poor law. In the archdeaconry, diocesan, probate and parish records the Bodleian holds most of the original sources for Oxfordshire genealogy. A duplicated leaflet giving further information about these can be obtained from the Department of Western Manuscripts.

At present the Bodleian also holds numerous Oxfordshire

collections of private papers deposited by their owners or by solicitors, most of them consisting mainly of deeds and in some instances other estate papers such as accounts and correspondence. Many of these were brought to light in the years immediately after the last war by the combined activities of Dr. W. O. Hassall, the Oxfordshire National Register of Archives Committee and the local Victoria County History Committee, and some were last-minute rescues from salvage. They were accepted by the Bodleian because the County Record Office had no room to accommodate them but most of them will eventually be transferred to that office. Meanwhile, some of the most notable of these family collections are those of the Berties, Earls of Abingdon; Brooks of Henley on Thames; Clerke-Brown of Aston Rowant; Croke of Studley; Dawkins of Over Norton; the Lords Harcourt; Risley, Barber and Cotton of north Oxfordshire; Lord Valentia; Weld; and Wykeham-Musgrave. Solicitors' deposits which comprise mainly similar papers of their clients' estates include the firms of Cooper and Caldecott of Henley, Morrell, Peel and Gamlen of Oxford and Marshall and Eldridge of Oxford. Other institutions who have similarly deposited their own records and title deeds include three Oxford colleges, All Souls, Christ Church and The Queen's (the two last have deposited only their medieval deeds), the borough of Henley on Thames, the Ewelme Charities, Hall's Brewery and the Oxford Methodist circuit. A very few similar collections are the Library's own property, acquired by gift or purchase, notably the large family collection of the Norths of Wroxton and most of the estate records of the Lovedays of Williamscote. There are typescript lists of all these family collections.

4. *Deeds and rolls.* The Bodleian contains very many Oxfordshire property deeds and a considerable number of manorial court rolls and accounts. Some of these are the Library's own property and of these many were acquired with other topographical material from antiquarian collectors from the time of Anthony Wood onwards. Wood's own large collection com-

prised mainly medieval monastic deeds and rolls including many from Oseney Abbey. Other Oxfordshire deeds, mainly post-medieval, make up the largest part of the private deposits mentioned above. It is the Library's practice to deal with all deeds and rolls in the same way, and to calendar and index them as a group apart from other manuscript material. All those acquired before 1878 are calendared and indexed in W. H. Turner and H. O. Coxe, *Calendar of charters and rolls preserved in the Bodleian Library* (1878), and those acquired since then are calendared in manuscript on slips. An index of persons mentioned in the Oxfordshire deeds owned by the Library and acquired since 1878, by W. O. Hassall, was published jointly by the Library and the Oxfordshire Record Society (vol. 44) in 1966. A card index of persons mentioned in most deposited deeds is available in the Library and there is also a card index of court rolls and other manorial documents arranged alphabetically by manors.

5. *Topographical views.* Some of the antiquarian collections mentioned above, notably those of Richard Gough, include 18th- and 19th-century drawings and engravings of Oxfordshire buildings and scenes and a few architectural plans. A few of the more recent acquisitions also include photographs, although the Library's biggest local collection of photographs, those of Henry Minn of Cassington (1870–1961), relate mainly to Oxford itself. Similar material has been bought in this century, notably a fine series of india ink drawings of Oxfordshire churches, with a few of other buildings, 1797–1830, by John Buckler (1770–1851) and his son John Chessell Buckler (1793–1894). (See plates 1–3.) The Library also has prints of all the photographs of Oxfordshire buildings taken for the Oxfordshire Architectural Record from 1956 onwards. A card index of Oxfordshire drawings, plans, prints and photographs arranged by parishes is available in Duke Humfrey.

6. *Maps.* Both printed and manuscript maps are cared for

by a separate department of the Library and are ordered and consulted in a special reading room furnished with large tables in the New Library. The Bodleian has copies of the early large-scale maps of the county of which the most important are those by Thomas Jefferys (1767), Richard Davis (1797) and A. Bryant (1824) and the first edition of the one-inch Ordnance Survey (1828–31). All editions of the 25-inch and 6-inch editions of the Ordnance Survey are also available for the whole county. There are some printed and manuscript Oxfordshire maps and plans among the Library's topographical collections, notably again those bequeathed by Richard Gough. Some deposited records also include estate maps and parish records include a few original enclosure maps. In the Map Room there is a card catalogue arranged by places which includes almost all these maps, and also a card index of the mapmakers represented.

The largest group of Oxfordshire manuscript maps in the Library is however the diocesan collection of tithe maps of *c*. 1838–48 (see plates 5–6). These maps and the awards rolled up with them were drawn up under the Tithe Commutation Act of 1836. They exist for all parishes in the county except those whose tithes had all been commuted before the passing of the act. Used in conjunction with the awards, these maps are a valuable record of land ownership and usage, and also a record of parish boundaries and a source for field names. The tithe maps are not included in the general Map Room card catalogue, but a duplicated list of them is available both in the Map Room and in Duke Humfrey.

To those who have not yet worked in the Bodleian the tracking down of all the material referred to here may seem a formidable task. Students looking for material on a particular Oxfordshire place or person should however eventually be able to find virtually everything in the Library likely to be of interest to them if they consult all the finding aids available. Those working on a particular subject will always find it more difficult to be sure they have explored all likely sources; the Bodleian does not provide subject indexes of its holdings. Staff with specialized knowledge of the Library's collections are, however, always willing to give what advice they can on where material on a specific subject might be found.

5. THE OXFORDSHIRE COUNTY RECORD OFFICE

Address and access: County Record Office, County Hall, New Road, Oxford, OX1 1ND. Tel. Oxford 49861, ext. 202. Open: 9.0 a.m. to 1.0 p.m., 2.0 p.m. to 5.0 p.m. on Mondays to Thursdays, and 9.0 a.m. to 1.0 p.m., 2.0 p.m. to 4.0 p.m. on Fridays. No reader's ticket required. Advance notice is required for the production of some records which are kept in a depository at Witney. Xerox copying is available.

The County Record Office was opened in 1936. Its primary function is to take charge of the records generated in the administration of the county, but it also collects and acts as a place of deposit for many kinds of local historical documents. A useful introduction to the scope of the records is *The Oxfordshire County Record Office and its records* by H. M. Walton (Record Publication no 1, reprinted from *Oxoniensia*, vol. III, 1938). They can conveniently be divided into five types.

1. *Quarter Sessions records.* Prior to the formation of County Councils in 1889 the county was largely administered by the Court of Quarter Sessions and its officer, the Clerk of the Peace. Records of Quarter Sessions exist for Oxfordshire from 1687 to 1972, and as elsewhere, especially until 1888, they contain both administrative and judicial material. The court met four times a year and its main record was its minute, or 'order', books, and the sessions 'rolls' or bundles of loose papers relating to the business of each session. These bundles contain information on the criminal cases before the court, and lists of prisoners and reports by the justices on the gaols. They also include presentments by parish officials and others on petty crimes in the parish and on such topics as the state of repair of roads and bridges; petitions for relief from distress of various kinds; papers

E

concerning the administration of the poor law and the treatment of indigent and vagrant members of the community; and regulations for clubs, societies, and meetings of dissenters and recusants including licences for their meeting houses and chapels. These are an important source for any local historian. Canon W. J. Oldfield calendared the bundles from 1687 to 1830; copies of his calendar are in the County Record Office and the Bodleian, and an index to the calendar is at the Record Office.

In the past documents produced by many legal transactions had to be deposited, enrolled or registered with the Clerk of the Peace. This has created certain classes of record important for local history. For Oxfordshire they include, for instance, nearly 200 enclosure awards, most of them with maps attached, falling mainly within the century from 1760 to 1860. These record the enclosure by act of parliament and re-allotment by commissioners of open fields, commons, greens, heaths and forests; and for the villages and manors which they cover they provide a splendid topographical record, including details of field systems, roads, landownership, and, in many cases, buildings. These are all listed in *A handlist of inclosure acts and awards relating to the county of Oxford* (Record Publication no. 2, 1963).

Another class of deposited record comprises plans of proposed railways, canals, turnpike roads, tramways and other public undertakings. Such plans had to be lodged with the Clerk of the Peace and they give a great deal of information on the land through which the undertaking passed. Because the plans were deposited at the parliamentary bill stage they include many schemes which were never in fact proceeded with and these are often extremely interesting. The railway plans are listed in *A handlist of plans, sections and books of reference for the proposed railways in Oxfordshire, 1825–36* (Record Publication no. 3, 1964). Other useful classes are assessments for the land tax from 1785 to 1832; poll books for disputed elections, and registers of electors after 1832; victuallers' recognizances from 1753 to 1822 which give names of inns and their licensees; rules of friendly societies; and registers of the estates of papists for the period from 1717 to 1788.

A good introduction to all these types of record is provided in the Historical Association pamphlet mentioned above (p. 33), F. G. Emmison and Irvine Gray, *County Records* (1967).

2. *County Council records.* The County Council came into existence on 1 April 1889 and ever since then it has been accumulating records of its many activities, such as the control of weights and measures, local taxation, licences, public health, planning, development, child care, welfare, education, libraries and the fire service. The papers created by these departments, the minute books of the committees, reports, byelaws, the deeds of the county's properties – all these are the records of the Council's activities and contain information invaluable to the local historian for the modern period. It should be noted however that many of the more recent records are confidential and are not yet open to the public or available for historical research.

3. *Other administrative records.* The Record Office also gathers in where possible the records of other administrative bodies (some of which are now defunct) or of other local government bodies. These include the records of boards of guardians of Poor Law Unions. Under the Reform Act of 1834 parishes were formed into unions to administer poor relief. These unions lasted for over a century and in their minute books and the records of the workhouses built by them can be found much information on the treatment of the poor. The Office holds the records of the unions based on Banbury, Bicester, Chipping Norton, Henley, Thame, Witney and Woodstock. It also holds some records of rural district councils, parish councils, highway boards and rural sanitary authorities. It should be remembered however that the ecclesiastical records of many parishes are housed at the Bodleian (see p. 49 above).

4. *Deposited collections.* The Record Office also holds many collections of private papers deposited by their owners. These complement those at present held on deposit in the Bodleian, and a guide to the collections deposited before 1966 is to be found in *Summary catalogue of the privately-deposited records in the Oxfordshire Record Office* (Record Publication no. 4, 1966). This lists some 360 collections; they include deeds, maps, manorial records, business records, estate papers and accounts, and personal papers from all parts of the county. Fuller guides and indexes to them can be consulted at the Office, and lists of more recent accessions are given in the quarterly Records Committee reports to the County Council.

The most noteworthy of these collections are the estate and family papers of the Lees and Dillons of Ditchley Park and Charlbury, of the Dashwood family of Kirtlington, and of the Earls of Jersey of Middleton Stoney. Other estates whose records are deposited include those of the Powys-Lybbe family of Hardwick, the Brownes of Kiddington, the Peers family of Chislehampton and the Willoughbys of Marsh Baldon. Large and old-established firms of solicitors, such as Messrs. Stockton, Sons and Fortescue of Banbury and Deddington, Aplin, Hunt, Thomas and Brooks of Banbury, Farrant and Sinden of Chipping Norton, Morrell, Peel and Gamlen of Oxford, and Cooper and Caldecott of Henley, have deposited very large collections of similar papers. The records of the two last firms are at present divided between the Bodleian and the Record Office.

Owners of records are of many other kinds and include businesses, charities and nonconformist societies and their chapels. Noteworthy amongst those who have deposited their records are the Banbury monthly meeting of Quakers, the Witney and Faringdon Methodist circuit, the Congregational chapel of Witney and the Baptist chapel of Hook Norton.

5. *The Davenport Library.* This extensive library, originally built up by former Clerks of the Peace, and named after

one of them, is devoted solely to Oxfordshire local history and to books concerned with the interpretation of documents. It has, in particular, a fine set of local directories. The Office also has long runs of the following local newspapers: *Jackson's Oxford Journal, The Oxford Journal Illustrated, The Oxford Times, The Oxford Chronicle, The Banbury Advertiser, The Chipping Norton Advertiser* and *The Witney Gazette.*

Material in private hands

There is still much raw material for Oxfordshire history in private hands within the county. Descendants of county families who still retain their estate records and other family papers at their homes are the Duke of Marlborough at Blenheim Palace, Lord Saye and Sele of Broughton Castle, Lord Macclesfield of Shirburn Castle, the Cottrell-Dormers of Rousham House and the Stonors of Stonor. Most Oxford colleges own some Oxfordshire property, and records of these estates (except the few deposited in the Bodleian, p. 50 above) are still held by the colleges themselves. Some of these include fine collections of medieval deeds and court rolls, early estate maps, surveys and accounts and long runs of leases. In some colleges these records are looked after by the college librarian or a specially designated archivist but in others they are the responsibility of the college bursar. Further details about the holdings of each college and the lists available can be found in Paul Morgan, *Oxford libraries outside the Bodleian* (1973).

At present only one Oxfordshire borough, Henley on Thames, and only one local district council, Bullingdon, has deposited its records, the former in the Bodleian and the latter in the County Record Office. Borough records of Banbury, Chipping Norton and Woodstock are in the custody of their respective town clerks; and some borough as well as charity, school and parish records for Burford are housed in the Tolsey Museum there. All the present urban and rural district councils should have preserved records of their administrative activities since 1894, and these are in the custody of the clerks to the respective councils. As these bodies are about to be replaced by larger districts under the Local Government Reorganization Act advice on obtaining access to their older records should now be sought from the County Record Office in the first instance.

Some Oxfordshire nonconformist churches still retain their own records, and this is especially true of the sects whose organization is least centralized such as the Congregationalists and Baptists. The extent to which the older Oxfordshire trades and industries have preserved their records has not yet been fully explored. A few businesses which are known to have interesting collections of papers include Charles Early and Marriott Ltd. of Witney and the Wolvercote Paper Mill. Finally there are many smaller collections of deeds, letters, bills, tradesmen's and farm account books, and antiquarian notes known to be scattered throughout the county in private houses; and doubtless there are others which have not yet come to the notice of those professionally interested.

The National Register of Archives was set up in 1945 to locate, preserve and record papers in private hands, and its central files and indexes at Quality House, Quality Court, off Chancery Lane, are now an invaluable guide to such material throughout the country. An Oxfordshire N.R.A. Committee was formed as a sub-committee of the Rural Community Council's Local History Committee in 1948. This body, especially in its early years, was responsible for listing many private Oxfordshire collections, and the committee's lists have been duplicated and circulated by the central N.R.A. office. Copies of almost all the Oxfordshire N.R.A. lists are available on open shelves in Duke Humfrey's Reading Room in the Bodleian, and many are also available in the County Record Office.

Anyone wishing to consult the records of a private family or institution should first find out whether there is an N.R.A. list of them. This will show the student whether the collection does in fact contain material likely to be of interest to him, and will also give the name and address of the person to whom he should write to obtain access to the papers. Many private owners are most generous in making their papers available on request in their own homes, but this is a courtesy which should never be taken for granted. The fact that an owner or an institution has allowed papers to be listed does not necessarily mean that they can be consulted just when it happens to be convenient for the student. Where there is no N.R.A. list, as for example in the case of some Oxford colleges, the Bodleian or the County Record Office may be able to advise both about the contents of a private collection and about its availability. Either repository would be very grateful to be informed when students discover and are able to examine material in private hands which has not been listed for the N.R.A.

There is much material which the student can seek out within his own village, especially if he wants to work on the history of his own parish. Although many parish records are now deposited in the Bodleian many others are still in parish chests or safes in the churches to which they relate. W. E. Tate's book, *The parish chest* (1969) fully describes the kind of material which can be found here. But in practice the results of examination of the contents of the chests may prove disappointing because the records which should be there have often been carelessly kept in the past, or deliberately discarded in the interests of tidiness. The contents of almost all Oxfordshire parish chests including those now deposited in the Bodleian were listed for the N.R.A. around 1950, and copies of the lists are available in the Bodleian and in some instances in the County Record Office. It is advisable to consult these lists before seeking permission to look at the parish records.

A careful study of the church building itself will always make a valuable contribution to parish history; monuments and inscriptions inside the church and headstones in the churchyard can serve not only to solve problems in family history, but to give indications of stability or change in the social structure of the community and to illustrate the taste and craftsmanship of succeeding generations. Many parishes have produced guides for visitors of widely differing scope and quality. Some printed handbooks can be bought at the City and County Museum bookstall, but many are available only in the church itself. Old parish magazines can sometimes be found in private hands and can be used to date restorations and alterations or gifts to the church.

If there is a primary school in the village, application for permission to consult the registers, log-books and inspectors' reports should be made to the headmaster or headmistress. Some of these records are however now deposited in the County Record Office and inquiries about the records of closed schools should also be made there. School archives give interesting information for the social historian, witnessing, for example, to the state of the children's health, the employment which they entered on leaving school, and the movement of families from rural parishes into Oxford.

The existing parish councils were established in 1894 and very rarely possess record material relating to parish administration before that date. Their council minute books and records of parish meetings should be available for consultation by students after 30 years have elapsed, and a few of these too are deposited in the County Record Office. Application should be made to the Chairman or Clerk of the Council.

In many Oxfordshire parishes groups such as Women's Institutes and old people's clubs or private individuals have entered for one of the scrap-book competitions arranged in recent years. Most of these scrap-books contain worthwhile information and copious illustrations; their value to the historian will appreciate over the years. Some of these scrap-books have been deposited in libraries for safe-keeping, but others are still kept in the villages by the societies or individuals who compiled them. The personal memoirs of older inhabitants whose lives have witnessed so many changes in the character of village life have in some cases been faithfully recorded; but the survival of written memoirs in the hands of their descendants is often precarious. It is important before it is too late to collect the memories of the generation now approaching old age; the use of a tape recorder is often convenient.

Older village people are often able to recall the field names in use when they were children and it is important to collect as many of these as possible before they are lost. The names remembered can then be compared with those surviving from earlier documentary sources. The latter are usually recorded in *The place-names of Oxfordshire, parts I and II*, by Margaret Gelling (English Place-name Society, vols. XXIII–IV, 1953–4).

Interest is growing in Victorian and Edwardian family photographs and in the picture post-cards, often of excellent quality, once sold in village shops. These record the appearance of the village before cottages were pulled down or modernized, roads widened and orchards built upon. They may also illustrate lost ways of country living. Such photographs are at risk when people move house or clear out their cupboards. The historian who makes use of them himself can perform a useful service in saving them from destruction. Owners who no longer want to keep their old photographs should be encouraged to offer them to one of the libraries with photographic collections. Owners who value their photographs and wish to keep them may be willing to lend them so that copies can be made and the negatives preserved.

III
Other Institutions Concerned With Oxfordshire History

Museums

A county with an old-established university city as its county town is likely to have a number of museums in it, and this is the case with Oxfordshire. Some of these museums, such as the Pitt-Rivers Museum in Parks Road, Oxford, are of a specialist nature with little immediately to interest the local historian; while others, although specialist, have some artefacts to concern him. Into this latter category would fall, for instance, the Museum of the History of Science in Broad Street, Oxford, which, amongst its rich collection of instruments, houses the Beeson collection of Oxfordshire clocks. The following are those of most relevance to local historians.

1. THE OXFORD CITY AND COUNTY MUSEUM

Address and access: Fletcher's House, Woodstock, Oxfordshire, OX7 1SN. Tel. Woodstock 811456. Open: During May to September 10.0 a.m. to 5.0 p.m. on Mondays to Fridays, 10.0 a.m. to 6.0 p.m. on Saturdays, and 2.0 p.m. to 6.0 p.m. on Sundays; during October to April 10.0 a.m. to 5.0 p.m. on Mondays to Saturdays.

The City and County Museum was founded in 1965 to collect material from the city and the county relevant to the history and environment of the people of the area and has been concentrating, initially, on the more immediate past. It occupies a handsome 18th-century house built round an Elizabethan core, although major expansion is planned in a separate branch for Oxford city and in the foundation of a rural museum on a farm site devoted to agriculture, craft and transport. Large local collections are being made in all these fields.

The Museum has many functions besides the collecting, restoring, documenting and displaying of objects from the past. Its Field Department promotes field studies and is building up an extensive record system to record sites, monuments and finds from prehistoric times to the 20th century and in this connection has a wide cover of air photographs. Any local historian interested in the sites and monuments in his area should seek the department's aid: while study groups and individuals are encouraged to help the department in its researches.

The Education Department operates a loan service of natural history, art, design and history specimens to schools. There are facilities for school groups or teachers' groups at the Museum.

The Museum issues an *Archaeological and Historical Newsletter* three times a year. Copies are distributed free to members of the Oxfordshire Architectural and Historical Society and to others on the Museum's mailing list; they can also be obtained from the Museum on request. This is an invaluable source of information about current activities, describing not only the exhibitions, lectures and field-work organized by the City and County Museum itself, but also the programmes of other interested bodies such as the Department for External Studies, the Ashmolean Museum, and many societies and groups. No one who wishes to keep abreast of developments in the field of local history and archaeology can afford to miss it.

The Museum also has a bookstall which is an excellent selling place for all local and archaeological material produced about the county, including pamphlets and guides.

2. THE ASHMOLEAN MUSEUM OF ART AND ARCHAEOLOGY

Address and access: Beaumont Street, Oxford, OX1 2PH. Tel. Oxford 57522. Open: 10.0 a.m. to 4.0 p.m. on weekdays, 2.0 p.m. to 4.0 p.m on Sundays.

The Museum was first opened in 1683 in the Old Ashmolean building in Broad Street, and is the oldest public museum in Great Britain. In the 19th century its collections were placed in the new University Galleries in Beaumont Street and in 1899 it assumed its present title of the Ashmolean Museum of Art and Archaeology. It is now a museum of international standing with important collections in the fine arts and antiquities.

The Department of Antiquities holds important local archaeological collections of all periods. The displays are to be found in the Evans Room (prehistoric), the Leeds Room (Roman and Saxon) and the Medieval Room. Reserve collections are available for study on application. Documentary sources include air photographs and papers relating to the collections.

The Museum Library is a university library and is not generally available for the public to use. The Library of the Oxfordshire Architectural and Historical Society is housed here: it is strong in local studies and is open only to members of the Society.

3. THE UNIVERSITY MUSEUM

Address and access: Parks Road, Oxford, OX1 3PW. Tel. Oxford 57467. Open: 10.0 a.m. to 4.0 p.m. on weekdays.

This Museum's main interest for local studies is in its collections and documentation of local geological materials.

4. BANBURY MUSEUM

Address and access: Marlborough Road, Banbury, Oxfordshire, OX16 8DF. Tel. Banbury 2282. Open: 10.0 a.m. to

1.0 p.m., 2.0 p.m. to 5.0 p.m. on Mondays and Wednesdays to Saturdays (closed on Tuesdays).

The Museum, which is in the same building as the Public Library, deals with various aspects of Banbury's life through the ages. It has geological, archaeological and historical collections. Part of the William Potts collection is in the Museum, and it also has a collection of old photographs of the Banbury area.

5. THE TOLSEY MUSEUM, BURFORD

Address and access: Burford, Oxfordshire. Open: during May to September, daily 2.30 p.m. to 5.0 p.m.

The Museum is housed in a 16th-century building standing on piers, the old Tolsey or customs house, and holds Burford's royal charters and some of the parish records. It displays the tools and work of local industries and crafts.

6. THE FILKINS AND BROUGHTON POGGS MUSEUM

Address and access: Filkins, Lechlade, Gloucestershire. Open: by arrangement with the curator.

This is a private museum owned by the curator, Mr. George Swinford, and is housed in two 17th-century cottages and the village lock-up. Its collections illustrate the folk-life of the village.

Oxford University Department for External Studies

The Department for External Studies (formerly the Delegacy for Extra-Mural Studies) plays an active part in local historical and archaeological activities. Apart from organizing a wide range of adult evening classes it now offers a three-year certificate course in British archaeology. During the year there are a series of day and weekend courses. One of these is organized in association with the Council for British Archaeology and another with the Oxford Archaeological Excavation Committee. During the summer the Department organizes an excavation and training school at Middleton Stoney. Anyone wishing to receive particulars of these courses should apply to the Director, Oxford University Department for External Studies, Rewley House, Wellington Square, Oxford, OX1 2JA, to be put on the Department's mailing list.

The Department publishes the Council for British Archaeology Group 9 Newsletter. Volumes 1, 1971 (15p.), 2, 1972 (40p.), and 3, 1973 (40p.), including postage, are still available. Early in 1973 the Department completed its involvement with the westward extension of the M40 by publishing an interim Report on the Group's activities. This report, *Archaeology and the M40 Motorway,* edited by R. T. Rowley and M. Davies, is available from the Director for 30p. including postage.

Local history societies

1. THE OXFORDSHIRE ARCHITECTURAL AND HISTORICAL SOCIETY

Since the amalgamation of the Oxford Architectural and Historical Society and the Oxfordshire Archaeological Society in 1972 to form the Oxfordshire Architectural and Historical Society there is now only this one Oxford society concerned with the local archaeology and history of the whole county. The history of the two societies which have been brought together is briefly outlined above (pp. 39–40) in connection with their publications. The Society also arranges evening lectures given at the Ashmolean Museum during University terms, and organizes full-day and half-day excursions. A sub-committee of the Society is concerned with listed buildings, and a Victorian group has recently been formed to promote the study of Victorian architecture and to restrain, if possible, the destruction of buildings of outstanding interest. Intending members should write to the Honorary Secretary, c/o Ashmolean Museum, Oxford, OX1 2PH.

2. OTHER LOCAL SOCIETIES

Informal groups tend to appear spontaneously wherever two or three are gathered together with a common interest in local history. Some of these are firmly rooted, but not all are long-lived. Some are revived after a lapse of years. It is difficult to ensure that any list of them is complete when it is made and most unlikely that it will long remain so. The City and County Museum *Newsletter* generally records the birth of new societies, the death of old ones, and the projects undertaken by the more active groups. Readers of the *Newsletter* will be in the best position to keep themselves informed about changes.

The following list does not include amenity societies. Although there is an obvious overlap in objectives and often in membership, the amenity societies have many interests which fall outside the scope of this handbook. All the societies listed below meet in the winter months for lectures and discussions on historical and archaeological subjects and arrange visits and excursions in summer. Any additional activities and any publications are noted below, with the names of the honorary secretaries from whom fuller information can be obtained about the time and place of meetings and the rate of subscriptions.

Banbury Historical Society. Miss C. G. Bloxham, Banbury Museum, Marlborough Rd., Banbury, OX16 8DF.

The Society takes part in archaeological digs and arranges historical exhibitions. Its important publications are described above (p. 41).

Bicester Local History Circle. Mr. T. Barnett, Layslett, Banbury Rd., Bicester.

Cassington History Society. Mr. R. J. Macrae, 16 The Tennis Ball Lane, Cassington, Oxford.

The society is organizing group projects on parish records, archaeology and vernacular architecture.

Chipping Norton Local History Society. Mr. David Eddershaw, Fenton House, Banbury Rd., Chipping Norton.

The Society has projects for collecting field names and tape recording memories of the old town.

Clanfield Historical Society. Mr. Fox-Russell, Pound Lane, Clanfield, Oxford.

Enstone Local History Circle. Miss D. Hutt, Meadowsgarth, Dean, Chadlington, Oxford.

Members meet in private houses and membership is restricted to 35. There is usually a short waiting list.

Eynsham Local History Group. Mrs. M. S. Howlett, Eynsham Mill, Eynsham, Oxford.

The Group published *Swinford Toll Bridge 1769–1969* by E. de Villiers (1969) and hopes to publish further occasional papers.

Goring Local History Society. Mr. H. B. Egerton, Thornhill, Fairfield Rd., Goring on Thames, Reading, RG8 0EX.

Kidlington and District Historical Society. Mr. J. O. Richards, 4 Orkney Place, Witney, OX8 6AU.

The Society issues a monthly newsletter to members, and has a history of Kidlington in preparation.

Littlemore Local History Society. Mr. T. H. White, 134 Herschel Crescent, Littlemore, Oxford.

The Society issues a Littlemore Journal three times a year.

South Oxfordshire Archaeological Group. Mrs. C. Graham Kerr, The Thatched Cottage, Whitchurch Hill, Oxfordshire.

The Group produce a monthly bulletin for members, and organize archaelogical digs and field meetings.

Standlake History Society. Mrs. J. Armstrong, Parsonage Close, Standlake, Witney, OX8 7QA.

The Woodstock Society's Local History Group. Miss Organ, Lynton Fields, Oxford Rd., Woodstock.

The Group are engaged in research into Old Woodstock's mayor-making ceremony and in an architectural survey of Woodstock.

IV
Some Questions Often Asked By Students of Local History

What subject can I work on?

1. This question may be asked by someone pursuing local history as a hobby, but more often it is asked by students who have to complete a piece of work, for example a college of education 'long essay', as an examination requirement. It is also sometimes a problem which presents itself to an organizer of an adult education class, a local history society or a school project. Whichever category you fall into, you should first consider your limitations, and exclude topics for which you do not have the time or qualifications, or for which the material is not easily accessible to you. You cannot work with medieval records without a knowledge of Latin. Do you read 16th- and 17th-century handwriting, or if not can you afford the time to acquire this skill? In fact this comes more quickly with practice than many beginners imagine. If you want to work mainly at home or at your place of meeting will it be possible to borrow reference works and obtain photocopies of original documents?

2. The whole of this handbook should help you in your choice of a subject. In the first section you will find references to gaps in our knowledge of the history of the county and suggestions of subjects which need further study on a regional basis. Throughout you will find references to the uses to which many kinds of material housed locally can be put. If you want to work on some aspect of the history of your own parish you will find advice on pages 59–61 above.

Further guidance on studying the history of families, houses and parish clergy is given below.

3. Many subjects become more interesting if studied over a wider area and much useful work is done by comparing conditions or developments in one part of the county with those in another, or elsewhere in other regions. A few of the many subjects suitable for this kind of treatment are the history of the various classes of society from the nobility to the poor, the history of trades and crafts, and of education, and many aspects of the history of agriculture and of the church. Railways, roads, canals, bridges, mills and many other kinds of buildings can be studied over the whole county or for a smaller area. If one of these subjects interests you you should first consult 'Cordeaux and Merry' (p. 35 above) to discover what work has been published on it for the county, and also see how it is dealt with parish by parish in the *Victoria County History* (pp. 37–9 above). You may only want to write an essay bringing together the information you collect from a variety of printed works. If you want to go further, first study the footnotes to find out what kinds of documentary materials are used in these printed works, and then inquire whether similar materials are available for another area which you could study in the same way. All the libraries and repositories described above will be especially glad to help you at this stage, that is when you have already done some work on what is easily available in print and can make your queries specific.

4. If you know you want to work with original records it is often less frustrating to begin by choosing some particular material rather than a subject to study, and this is especially true of work with a group. To give just a few examples, this could be some family correspondence, a diary, a collection of poor law documents, household or estate accounts and vouchers, an estate, enclosure or tithe map and survey, census returns or wills and probate inventories for a particular class of persons or a particular place. If you begin working on an interesting document or collection of papers you will find that the subjects which it illuminates suggest themselves.

You should make sure, again with the help of 'Cordeaux and Merry', that you have first looked at any work which has already appeared in print based on the material you propose to use so that you are not merely duplicating the work of others. Here again, the libraries and the County Record Office may be able to guide you to suitable material and to aids to interpreting it, and also help to prevent you repeating work which has already been done.

5. In all the above suggestions it is assumed that you intend to produce an essay, article or book on your chosen subject or material. There are however many devoted students of local history who are content to transcribe, calendar or index records, and do not seek to interpret the material they handle. Such work is invaluable especially when it can be made available to others by placing the copy, list or index in a library or the Record Office. It is particularly useful to make complete copies of unique material which is not housed in a public repository. You may be willing and able to transcribe and index your parish registers or other interesting parish records such as churchwardens' accounts. You may know of letters, a diary or memoirs in private hands which the owner does not want to part with but would allow you to copy. Some interesting classes of record often at risk such as loose poor law papers or property deeds contain more common form and so lend themselves to calendars or lists rather than to complete copies. Most record repositories can see the need for various detailed lists and indexes of material in their custody which they know their own staff will never have time to compile. They usually welcome voluntary help, especially if the volunteer has clear handwriting and works accurately, and inquiries should be made at the Bodleian and the Record Office.

How can I trace the history of my family?

Many of those who search local records for genealogical purposes probably do not think of themselves as students of local history but they are some of the inquirers this handbook seeks to help. If your family lived in the same area for long periods you can hope eventually to trace a continuous line back to the first half of the 16th century. You are not likely to get much further back than this unless the family was a landed one of at least gentry status. Only material for Oxfordshire family history is dealt with here. Much more detailed information relating to the whole country will be found in David E. Gardner and Frank Smith's *Genealogical research in England and Wales*, volumes 1 and 2 (Salt Lake City, 1956, 1959).

1. Most people can trace their family back for two or three generations from what their older relatives can tell them, and from old birth, marriage and death certificates or other family papers. It is also likely that from family hearsay you will at least know where your family was living longer ago than this. These facts and traditions are your starting point and you will need to work backwards from them. Civil registration of births, marriages and deaths was introduced by act of Parliament in 1837, and in theory you should be able to trace your family back to that date from the records kept in accordance with this act by the Registrar-General at Somerset House in London. These civil records are however sometimes incomplete up to the middle of the 19th century; fees are payable for searching them; and unless the exact date of a birth, death or marriage is known the search is likely to be extensive and therefore costly because of the great bulk of the records.

2. Thus you will probably find it more convenient to go immediately to the parish registers of baptisms, marriages and burials for the places where your family has lived. The clergy have been required to keep such registers since 1538, and for many Oxfordshire parishes they begin sometime in the 16th century. These registers may be deposited in the Bodleian Library, or they may still be in the custody of the incumbent of the parish. If the registers you need to search are still with the incumbent you will find his name, address and telephone number in the current *Oxford Diocesan Year Book*. In asking to be allowed to consult such registers you

should give reasonable notice, and be prepared to pay the fixed scale of fees which the clergy are entitled to charge for this purpose.

3. From 1604 onwards the clergy were required to send into the diocesan registry annual transcripts of all the year's entries in their registers. For most Oxfordshire parishes these 'bishops' transcripts', also in the Bodleian, have only survived from about 1720 onwards. Usually, however, they continue to the third quarter of the 19th century, and for this 150 years it is often convenient to use these transcripts if the original registers are not also in the Bodleian. The Library also has some modern copies and indexes of registers.

4. If your family does not appear in the registers of the parish where you know they were living, or if some generations seem to be missing, this is likely to be because they were Roman Catholics or Protestant nonconformists. These churches have kept their own records of births or baptisms, marriages and deaths or burials from the 17th century onwards although few have survived earlier than about 1700. Some are still with the clergy or officials of the individual churches or chapels, some are deposited in the County Record Office or the Bodleian, and some have been collected up centrally and are now in the Public Record Office. Detailed information about the pre-1837 registers of every Oxfordshire parish is given in volume V of the *National index of parish registers*, 'South Midlands and Welsh Border' by D. J. Steel (Society of Genealogists, 1966). From this volume you will find the periods for which the registers and bishops' transcripts of each parish have survived, whether the registers were still with the incumbent in 1966, whether any printed or manuscript copies are available elsewhere, and the whereabouts and dates of any surviving catholic or nonconformist registers.

5. The other main source for family history is wills and grants of administrations to the relatives of persons who died without leaving a will. Probate was the concern of ecclesiastical courts until 1857, and all the Oxfordshire wills proved in local courts and all the records of administrations granted

there are now in the Bodleian. These wills and administrations go back to the early 16th century and complete indexes of persons are available in the Library. But many wealthier people and all those owning property in more than one diocese had their wills proved in the Prerogative Court of the Archbishop of Canterbury, and these, going back to 1383, are now housed in the Public Record Office in London. Printed indexes of these 'P.C.C.' wills down to 1700 have been published by the British Record Society and are available on open shelves in the Bodleian.

6. Marriages can be difficult to trace because they often did not take place in the bridegroom's parish, and often you will not know the bride's maiden name or parish. Registers of banns giving these details sometimes survive from 1754 and more often from 1823, and you should look out for these amongst parish registers. More people were married by licence in previous centuries than at present, and in Oxfordshire such licences could be obtained from either the bishop or the archdeacon. The bonds and affidavits which the bridegroom or the couple's relatives were required to give when applying for a licence have survived from 1660 for both types of licence and these are also now in the Bodleian, with indexes. A marriage bond or affidavit will almost always give you the parishes of both parties and show where the marriage was to take place. You may also be given the ages of both bride and bridegroom (although this is often given just as '21 and upwards'), and if either party is a minor there may be references to a named parent giving consent to the marriage. A bondsman of the same surname as the bride is likely to be her father. The Bodleian has very recently been given another invaluable source for tracing marriages. This is a combined index of some of the marriage registers of about 100 Oxfordshire parishes, the majority of them in north Oxfordshire, compiled by Mr. J. S. W. Gibson.

7. Most of the basic documentary sources for Oxfordshire genealogy are thus now in the Bodleian, and anyone beginning a search should ask for the Library's leaflet mentioned above (p. 49). This gives full details of the indexes available,

and also information about similar material in the Library and elsewhere relating to the adjacent counties of Berkshire and Buckinghamshire.

8. There are many other sources to which you can turn when you lose track of your family in registers, wills and marriage bonds. If you know where a person was living in 1861 or 1851, but not where he came from originally, you should consult the census returns of those years on microfilm in the Oxford City Library (p. 44 above) as these normally give the ages and places of birth of everyone listed. Other classes of record will only give you further clues as to when a person moved into the parish in which you have been searching, or lead you to other places where the same surname is found. From such clues, however, you will be able to go on again to the registers of another parish and look again at more wills and marriage records to establish relationships. Meanwhile too you will be filling out the bare pedigree with further biographical information. Almost any class of local record in print or manuscript for which a persons index exists is worth trying and in particular you should turn to the general persons index of many of their collections maintained by the County Record Office and to the indexes of persons mentioned in deeds in the Bodleian Library.

9. Many of the records which contain lists of names arranged by parishes have not however been indexed by persons, and only if you are very persistent will you be willing to read through such records for the whole county in the hope of finding a mention of your surname. But if you want to follow up a clue to a particular parish, or just want to obtain further information about the family, it would be worth trying any of the following. In the Oxfordshire directories, listed in 'Cordeaux and Merry' (see p. 35 above) on pages 146–7, you will find all the principal householders listed by parishes from the mid-19th century onwards. Annual registers of parliamentary electors are available from 1833 onwards, and there are also printed poll books listing the smaller numbers of persons entitled to vote in the county elections of 1754, 1826, 1830 and 1831. Ratepayers will be

listed in any records of poor, church or highway rates which may survive among parish records from the late 16th to the 19th centuries. Manorial court rolls (see plate 4) can be of any period from the 13th to the 19th century and these contain many names and record changes in the tenure of manorial lands which often give clues about the date of the holder's death. Manorial surveys from the 16th century onwards, enclosure awards of about 1760 to 1860 in the County Record Office, and tithe awards of the 1840s in the Bodleian Library will all list owners of land, and often also the occupiers of all the properties in the parish or manor. All types of taxation records consist of lists of names, usually arranged by parishes, with details of the sums owed, but most of these are in the Public Record Office. An important class among Quarter Sessions records in the County Record Office is however the assessments to the land tax which survive for the period 1785 to 1832. Hearth tax returns of 1665 for the whole county are printed as volume 21 of the Oxfordshire Record Society (1940).

How old is my house and what is its history?

A house of any antiquity at all is an obvious and visible survival from the past, and it is easy to think that its history must therefore be equally obvious and accessible. But this is not so. More often than not the task of tracing the history of a house is about the most difficult of all local historical projects. Do not therefore be disappointed if you can find virtually nothing about your house in the past: there are thousands more like you. But if you are setting out to try to discover the history of your house, there are certain obvious steps to take, and these are outlined here.

1. The technique should always be to work backwards from the present. Look at your house, its position and its architecture. How old does it seem to be? There are books to help you, and a useful primer is David Iredale, *This old house* (Shire Publications, 1968) which gives much useful

information on the sorts of records which may prove useful, and mentions other helpful books. The City and County Museum may be able to suggest someone to advise you on architectural details. Buildings of great antiquity or of special architectural merit are listed by the Ministry of Housing and Local Government. The Ministry's list ascribes approximate dates to the various parts of each house it includes, based mainly on architectural evidence. Copies of the Oxfordshire lists are available in the Bodleian Library and at the County Record Office. Once you know the approximate age of your house you know how far back you have to go in your research.

2. Your next step should be to consult printed local sources to see if the house is mentioned in them: the *Victoria County History* (see p. 37 above) and other histories of your locality of which you know or which are listed in 'Cordeaux and Merry' (see p. 35 above). The Post Office, Kelly's and other county Directories going back to the mid-19th century may well help you to pin-point your house.

3. At an early stage you should also turn to maps. By working backwards through the various editions and revisions of the Ordnance Survey maps it is possible to narrow the period when your house was built or enlarged if it is less than 100 years old. The most useful for this purpose are the 6-inch survey, the 25-inch survey and the 1/500 town survey. The most valuable of all maps if your house is more than 100 years old are the tithe maps of the 1840s in the Bodleian Library. From these and the awards rolled up with them you can find details of the owner and the occupier and of the land which went with the house in that decade (see p. 52 above and plates 5–6). The enclosure maps in the County Record Office are not always so useful for this purpose but they may show your house, and if it is a farmhouse you may be able to deduce that it was newly built as a result of enclosure. If it is close to a railway, canal, gasworks or similar public undertaking built after 1792, the deposited plan of that undertaking amongst the Quarter Sessions records in the County Record Office should show it and give you the name of the

owner and occupier at that date. Both the Bodleian Library and the County Record Office have large numbers of maps of estates from the 17th century onwards: you may be fortunate enough to find a map of the estate of which your house once formed part. Auction catalogues of individual properties and large estates often contain maps and particulars of individual houses, and many of these again are listed is 'Cordeaux and Merry'.

4. If the deeds of your house are in the possession of yourself or your solicitor, go through them as far back as they go. They may not go back far since the change in the need for evidence of title made by the 1925 Law of Property Act meant that many deeds were disposed of. But they will at least give you the names of some former owners, perhaps trace the origins of your house back to some large estate which was broken up, and at best give you all the answers you are looking for. Deeds referring to your property may have found their way into one of the local repositories amongst papers from a solicitor's office or the records of a large estate.

5. If your house is a special one in some way, then there are certain special sorts of records to which you can turn. If it was once a parsonage house several classes of the diocesan records in the Bodleian Library, especially glebe terriers and Queen Anne's Bounty mortgage papers, will be likely to give you further information. If your house was ever a public house, a school, a workhouse or a tollhouse there may well be material relating to it in the County Record Office. The staff either there or at the Bodleian will be glad to give you advice on specialised classes of records to search for these and other particular types of buildings.

6. If your house is not a special one and you have no deeds to give you a lead, you will need to explore any sources which will give you the names of further former owners and occupiers. These include the various types of record which list names by parishes mentioned in connection with family history on pages 76–7 above, such as census returns, rate books, electoral registers, hearth tax and land tax returns and manorial surveys and rentals. It is however at this point

that your search may become frustrating, because it is often not possible to know which of the persons named was in fact the past occupant of your house.

7. If however you can find some names of people who either lived in or owned the house you can then go on to other records concerning those people which may give you other information about the house. People are easier to trace than properties, and if you find you want to pursue a particular family of owners or occupiers the whole of the previous section on family history should help you. If the house was owned at some time by an Oxford college it is likely that you will find references to it in college archives (see p. 57 above). These may be past leases of the property, or references in rent account books, and there may also be maps there. If your house was once part of a large family estate, similar records may survive for that estate. If it was once copyhold of a manor manorial court rolls, if they survive, could be a great help to you. Your house may stand on what was charity land, or have been a charity property; it may once have belonged to a corporation or borough. The County Record Office or the Bodleian Library will probably be able to tell you whether the records of these bodies are known to survive for the place in which you are interested.

8. You may be able to find wills for some owners or occupiers of your house amongst the Oxfordshire wills proved locally now deposited in the Bodleian Library (p. 49 above). Wills often mention property, and sometimes give clues as to who the former owners or landlords were. From Elizabethan times to the early 18th century these wills are often accompanied by probate inventories, and some inventories list the deceased person's goods room by room. A detailed inventory of this kind is invaluable evidence about the size and shape of a house.

How can I compile a list of incumbents of my parish church?

For most ancient Oxfordshire parishes it is possible to

compile almost complete lists of rectors or vicars from the 13th century to the present day. Their names and dates are obtained from the records of institutions to benefices found in bishops' registers. These records usually give the name of the patron presenting the incumbent, the cause of vacancy, and the name of the previous incumbent, as well as the exact date of institution and the name and status or degree of the new man. You should if possible include all these details in your list, rather than giving just the year of institution.

1. In the Middle Ages Oxfordshire was an archdeaconry in the large diocese of Lincoln and for that period these institution records are therefore included in the Lincoln bishops' registers now deposited with all the other Lincoln diocesan records in the Lincolnshire Archives Office, The Castle, Lincoln. The registers relate to the whole diocese and record institutions in chronological order, sometimes mixed with other acts of the bishop, so it is a considerable task to extract all the references to one benefice, even if you have some knowledge of Latin and medieval handwriting. This work has however already been done for all the Oxfordshire parishes so far included in the *Victoria County History* (see pp. 37–8 above), and typescript lists of medieval incumbents for these parishes are available in the Bodleian Library. If your parish is not included here you will need to consult the original records at Lincoln, or employ a qualified person to do this for you.

2. From 1542 these records of institution are continued in the Oxford bishops' registers among the diocesan records deposited in the Bodleian Library. Canon Oldfield's index of these, his 'Clerus' mentioned on p. 49 above, provides nearly complete lists of incumbents for most Oxfordshire parishes from 1542 onwards, but you will need to look up the original registers to find the patrons' names. The Oxford diocesan records also include presentation deeds in which patrons presented their candidates to the bishop for institution, and resignation deeds by which clergy resign their benefices. There are typescript calendars of these available

on open shelves in the Bodleian which are worth consulting
where there are gaps in the lists in the 'Clerus'.

3. Diocesan and archdeaconry visitation 'call books', that
is lists of clergy and churchwardens with notes of their
attendances at visitations, are also useful for filling gaps.
These extend from 1578 to the mid-19th century although
both the diocesan and the archidiaconal series are incomplete.
Gaps most often occur during the reign of Elizabeth I when
the see was vacant for long periods. The succession of clergy
during this reign has however been worked out for most
parishes by S. S. Pearce in a series of articles arranged by
rural deaneries in the *Oxfordshire Archaeological Society
Reports*, 1912–1920. There may also be gaps during the Civil
War and Commonwealth periods when diocesan administration broke down. If your parish had an incumbent deprived
either as a royalist or for not conforming in 1660–2 you will
find details of these men's careers in A. G. Matthews, *Walker
Revised* (1948) and *Calamy Revised* (1934). Parish registers
and clergy's wills may also help to fill gaps. As many clergy
were Oxford or Cambridge graduates it is always worth consulting J. Foster's *Alumni Oxonienses* (1891–2) or J. and
J. A. Venn's *Alumni Cantabrigienses* (1922–54) if you know
an incumbent's name but not the year of his institution.

4. A few ancient parishes with poor endowments for the
incumbent have always been served only by curates, and
within some parishes there have been since the Middle Ages
separate chapels of ease also served by curates. Dorchester
for example has always been only a curacy, and Woodstock
has always been a chapel of ease in Bladon parish. For such
places it is much more difficult to work out the succession of
incumbents. It is unlikely that more than one or two medieval
names will be recovered from chance references in the
Lincoln diocesan records or elsewhere. Curates are licensed,
not instituted, and records of these licences are only included
in the Oxford bishops' registers from the late 18th century
onwards. The Oxford diocesan records include some earlier
nominations to curacies and from 1604 onwards some subscriptions of conformity which curates were required to

make when they were licensed. Some 17th- and 18th-century curates' names have been added to the 'Clerus' from these sources. The 'call books' mentioned above also include curates as well as rectors and vicars. Again parish registers and wills may provide further names, and sometimes they will show that the curate whose name is known from another source continued to serve the parish until he died and was buried there.